I0003389

HELP!!!

A Beginners Guide To:

Windows 10

Written by Richard Hawkins

Published by IGT Publishing

Copyright © 2016 IGT Publishing
All rights reserved. No part of this book shall be reproduced, stored in a retrieval system, or transmitted by any means, electronic, mechanical, recording, photocopying, or otherwise, without the prior written permission of the publisher.

Notice of Liability
A great deal of effort has gone into ensuring that the content of this book is both accurate and up to date. However, IGT Publishing and the author will not be held liable for any loss or damage from the use of the information herein.

Trademarks
All trademarks are acknowledged as belonging to their respective companies.

Introduction to Windows 10

Getting Started With Windows 10

Windows Basics

File Explorer

Working with Files and Folders

Windows 10 Apps

Networking

Customizing Windows

The Internet

Email

Pictures, Video and Audio

Security

Troubleshooting and Maintenance

Index

CHAPTER 1

Introduction to Windows 10

We begin by taking a look at the new features in Windows 10, such as Cortana, Microsoft's personal assistant, the Edge browser, and Virtual desktops. We also see what is no longer in Windows – a number of features that were present in Windows 8 have been removed in Windows 10.

For those of you who have yet to buy Windows 10, we explain everything you need to know with regard to this decision – which edition to get, establishing whether or not your PC can run Windows 10, and more.

Introduction

So, here we are again – back on the merry-go-round. Microsoft has released yet another edition of its Windows operating system to replace the unlamented and almost universally unpopular Windows 8. Windows 10 is the name given to this one and one of the main design aims has been to bridge the gap between computers and tablets without alienating users of either.

A feature that clearly demonstrates this is the way that a two-in-one device, such as Microsoft's Surface Pro 3, automatically switches between computer mode and tablet mode whenever a keyboard is attached or unattached.

The new operating system corrects the mistakes made in Windows 8 by taking the best parts of previous Windows editions and combining them with some new features to create a cohesive package that is a considerable improvement in nearly every respect.

Another plus is that the upgrade process is straightforward and, providing they are prepared to wait for it, is free for most non-corporate users of Windows 7 and 8.

The introduction of Windows 10 also confirms the direction that Microsoft is taking with Windows. It brings an end to the grand and dramatic changes seen in recent editions and replaces them with small and more subtle tweaks similar to those seen on Android and iOS smartphones and tablets. Expect to see this trend continue in the future.

First impressions suggest Windows 10 will be the dual-purpose operating system that Microsoft intended Windows 8 to be but wasn't. Furthermore, it provides the groundwork for future Windows editions that will be able to run effortlessly on whatever type of device the manufacturers can dream up. It won't just be dual-purpose but triple-purpose and more.

This comes later though. What Microsoft is offering right now with Windows 10 is a fast, well featured and functional operating system that is equally at home on a tablet or smartphone as it is on a desktop computer. Apple have been doing it for years with iOS; Microsoft are finally catching up.

If you're running Windows 7 or Windows 8, you've got absolutely nothing lose and quite a bit to gain by making the jump to Windows 10. If you're still on Windows XP, well, you've probably got your reasons.

Windows 8 and Windows 10 have been the initial steps in a transition from operating system to ecosystem. This is Microsoft's second attempt at bringing us the future, and while it is still not perfect, this time it's a lot closer to reality.

What's New in Windows 10?

With Windows 10 sees a raft of new features, plus the return of some discarded in Windows 8. In no particular order, they are:

Start Menu
Windows 10 returns the Start menu to its position at the lower left-hand corner of the desktop. The Windows 10 Start menu incorporates a bit of the Metro Start screen's functionality by making it possible to also have live tiles.

Rejigged Metro Apps
The Metro apps in Windows 8 opened full screen and offered no options. In Windows 10, they can be resized, moved, and have a toolbar of options

Cortana
Cortana is a personal assistant that finds information for you. It can search online, your computer, OneDrive, and business networks, for files using filters, such as "Find pictures from June." It can also carry out actions, such as playing music, setting alarms, creating reminders and much more.

Edge Browser
Edge is a brand new browser that is slick and speedy in operation. It comes with some interesting features such as Reading View and Hub. It is also tightly integrated with Cortana and so can be controlled by the personal assistant.

Virtual Desktops
Virtual desktops is a feature intended for power users and makes it possible to instantly switch between multiple virtual desktops all running different apps

Action Center
This replaces the Notifications feature in Windows 8. It also provides controls for common functions, such as activating Bluetooth or Tablet mode.

Continuum Mode
For touchscreen users, Continuum dynamically switches the interface between the computer-friendly desktop and a Windows 8-like mode that's better suited for fingers, depending on how you're using the device.

Windows Hello
Windows Hello is a security feature that lets you sign into your computer with just your face or finger. It works by scanning your face, iris, or fingerprint to unlock devices and does away with the need for a password or pin number

Universal Apps
A number of apps including Photos, Videos, Music, Maps, People, Mail and Calendar will look and feel the same across different devices and screen sizes. Their data will also be saved and synced automatically via OneDrive.

What's Gone In Windows 10?

When Microsoft give with one hand, they take with the other. Windows 10 may come with some nifty new features but it also loses some provided in Windows 7 and 8. They include:

Windows Media Center

If you have Windows 7 Home Premium, Windows 7 Professional, Windows 7 Ultimate, Windows 8 Pro with Media Center, or Windows 8.1 Pro with Media Center and you install Windows 10, Windows Media Center will be removed.

DVD Playback

With no support provided in Windows 10, you have no choice but to look elsewhere. Fortunately, there are plenty of free third-party software packs available, such as the VLC media player. For more fully-featured players, try CyberLink PowerDVD and Corel WinDVD.

Desktop Gadgets

Gadgets are mini-programs, which offer information at a glance and provide easy access to frequently used tools. Supplied with Windows 7, they included a Calendar, Clock, Weather, Feed Headlines, Slide Show, and Picture Puzzle.

Solitaire, Minesweeper and Hearts

The Solitaire, Minesweeper, and Hearts games that come pre-installed on Windows 7 will be removed when you upgrade to Windows 10. All Microsoft's card games are now available through the Microsoft Solitaire Collection, which is a single app that's installed by default. Minesweeper, however, has to be downloaded from the Windows Store.

Floppy Drive Support

Are you really still using a floppy drive? Well, if so, you will now have to download the latest driver from Windows Update or directly from the manufacturer's website.

Windows Updates

Windows 10 Home users lose the ability to update Windows manually; it's now done automatically and there is no way to change this. However, Windows 10 Pro and Enterprise users will be able to defer updates.

Windows Essentials OneDrive App

If you have Windows Live Essentials on your computer and upgrade to Windows 10, the OneDrive App will be replaced by the OneDrive Inbox, which combines email and OneDrive storage automatically.

For everyone else, Windows 10 has a default email application built in, and OneDrive file access is integrated into Windows Explorer, automatically synchronizing files you copy to the folder to your free cloud storage account.

Editions of Windows 10

Windows 10 comes in a number of editions that are tailored to different uses and users:

Windows 10 Home

Windows 10 Home is the consumer-focused desktop edition of Windows and is designed for the average user who has no need for the more advanced features and functionality found in the other editions. Accordingly, it is the lowest priced edition of Windows 10.

Windows 10 Pro

Windows 10 Pro is an advanced version of Windows 10 Home and comes with a range of extra features intended to meet the diverse needs of small businesses. Amongst many other things, it lets customers take advantage of the new Windows Update for Business, which reduces management costs, provides controls over update deployment, and offers quick access to security updates.

Windows 10 Mobile

Windows 10 Mobile is designed for use on mobile, touch-centric devices like smartphones and tablets. It offers the same, new universal Windows apps that are included in Windows 10 Home, as well as the new touch-optimized version of Microsoft Office.

Windows 10 Enterprise

Windows 10 Enterprise builds on Windows 10 Pro, adding advanced features designed to meet the demands of medium and large sized organizations. It provides advanced capabilities to help protect against the ever-growing range of modern security threats targeted at devices, identities, applications and sensitive company information. It also supports the broadest range of options for operating system deployment and comprehensive device and app management.

Windows 10 Mobile Enterprise

Windows 10 Mobile Enterprise is designed for business customers to use on smartphones and small tablets. It offers the same productivity, security and mobile device management capabilities that Windows 10 Mobile provides, and adds flexible ways for businesses to manage updates. In addition, Windows 10 Mobile Enterprise will incorporate the latest security and innovation features as soon as they are available.

Windows 10 Education

Windows 10 Education is designed to meet the needs of schools – staff, administrators, teachers and students. This edition will be available through academic Volume Licensing, and there will be paths for schools and students using Windows 10 Home and Windows 10 Pro devices to upgrade to Windows 10 Education.

Can My Computer Run Windows 10?

Traditionally, every edition of Windows has required more in the way of hardware resources than the editions that preceded it. This trend came to a stop with Windows 7, which ran perfectly well on the same hardware that its predecessor, Windows Vista, did.

This has continued with Windows 10, so users upgrading from Windows Vista, Windows 7 or Windows 8 do not also have to upgrade their computer.

The official system requirements of Windows 10 are:

- **Processor** – 1GHz or faster

- **Memory (RAM)** – 1GB (32-bit) or 2GB (64-bit)

- **Disk space** – 16GB (32-bit) or 20GB (64-bit)

- **Graphics** – Microsoft DirectX 9 with WDDM driver

- **Display** – 800 x 600

Please note, however, that the above is the absolute minimum required. While Windows 10 will run on this hardware, it may not do so particularly well. To be more specific, it will probably be on the slow side, and if you run resource-intensive software such as 3D games, Photoshop, etc, it may struggle to cope.

If you wish to avoid this, our recommendation is to install twice the recommended amount of memory, i.e. 2GB on a 32-bit system and 4GB on a 64-bit system. It also has to be said that a 1Ghz processor is very slow and out-dated by today's standards. If this is what you have in your PC, or similar, it could well be time to buy a new computer.

In addition, the following will be required to use some features:

- **Windows Hello** – an infrared camera for facial recognition or iris detection, or a fingerprint reader

- **BitLocker To Go** – a USB drive (Windows 10 Pro only)

- **Hyper-V** – a 64-bit system with second level address translation (SLAT) capabilities and an additional 2GB of memory

- **Wi-Fi Direct Printing** – a Wi-Fi adapter that supports Wi-Fi Direct and a device that supports Wi-Fi Direct Printing

- **DVD playback** – DVD playback software

- **Speech Recognition** – a high fidelity microphone array or a hardware driver with microphone array geometry exposed

Which Edition of Windows Do I Have?

Depending on which edition of Windows 10 you want to buy, you may need to know your current edition. To do this:

1. On the keyboard, tap the **Windows** key (bottom-left) and the **E** key simultaneously

2. File Explorer will open

3. Right-click on an empty area of the window and click **Properties**

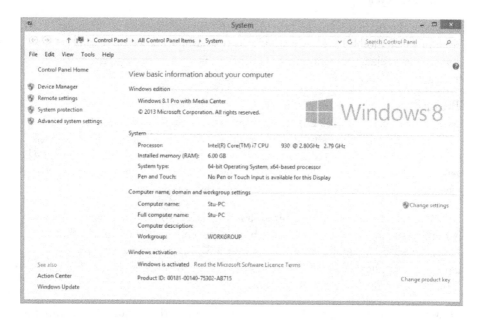

4. At the top, under **Windows edition,** you will see the edition installed on the computer

Looking further down under **System,** you will see details regarding the processor and the amount of installed memory. As we explained on page 12, this is information you may need to know in order to ensure your computer can run not just your new edition of Windows but also the programs you intend to use with it.

System type will tell you if your current edition of Windows is 32-bit or 64-bit. This is something else you may need to know as we explain on the next page.

You will also be asked when upgrading to Windows 10 to specify whether you want the 32-bit or 64-bit version.

32-Bit Versus 64-Bit

All modern CPUs support 64-bit architecture. But what is it and how does it benefit the user?

The term "64-bit" when used in reference to a processor, or CPU as they are known, means that in one integer register the CPU can store 64 bits of data. Older CPUs, which could only support 32-bit architecture, could store only 32 bits of data in a register, i.e. half the amount. Therefore, 64-bit architecture provides better overall system performance as it can handle twice as much data in one clock cycle.

However, the main advantage provided by 64-bit architecture is the huge amount of memory it can support. CPUs operating on a 32-bit Windows system can utilize a maximum of 4GB, whereas on a 64-bit system they can utilize up to 192GB.

The caveat is that a 64-bit system requires all the software to be 64-bit compatible, i.e. it must be 64-bit software. This includes the operating system and device drivers (this is why more recent versions of Windows [XP, Vista, 7, 8.1, and now Windows 10] are supplied in both 32-bit [x86] and 64-bit [x64] versions). Note that most 32-bit software will run on a 64-bit system but the advantages provided by 64-bit architecture won't be available.

So who will benefit from a 64-bit system and who won't? The simple answer is that every computer user will benefit as their system will be more efficient. Don't expect to see major speed gains over a 32-bit system when running day-to-day applications such as web browsers, word processing and 2D games, though; you probably won't notice any.

However, when running CPU-intensive applications that require large amounts of data to be handled, e.g. video editing, 3D games, computer aided design (CAD) etc, 64-bit systems will be considerably faster. Also, if you need more memory than the current limit of 4GB possible with a 32-bit system, 64-bit architecture allows you to install as much as you want (up to the limitations of the motherboard).

Users who install Windows 10 Pro will have access to a virtualization utility called Hyper-V that enables "virtual computers" to be built on the computer. One of the requirements for building virtual PCs with Hyper-V is that the computer must be running on 64-bit architecture.

So when the upgrade procedure asks which one you want to install, opt for the 64-bit version of Windows 10 – there is really no reason not to.

Upgrading to Windows 10

The Windows 10 upgrade procedure is as follows:

1. Having paid for Windows 10, you are asked to select either the 32-bit or 64-bit version of the **Download Tool Now**

2. You are then asked if you want to **Upgrade this PC now** or **Create installation media for another PC**

Upgrade this PC now
If you're not sure what you're doing, select the Upgrade this PC now option. This is the easiest way to do it as Windows 10 is simply downloaded to the computer and installed over the top of the existing installation.

When the download is complete, you will see a number of screens such as **Creating Windows 10 media** and **Getting updates** but the only time you have to do anything is at the Accept License Terms screen where you will have to click **Accept**.

Then, you will see the Upgrading Windows screen shown below:

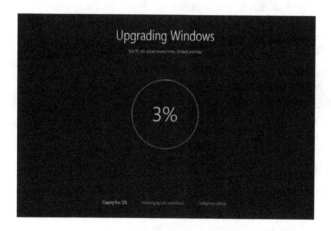

Following this, depending on your upgrade route, you may be asked to validate your copy of Windows 10 by entering the product key. Some setting up screens will follow, such as **Getting things ready** before, finally, you see the Windows 10 desktop

Create installation media for another PC
This option, which is intended for more advanced users, lets you download the Windows 10 setup files to a location of your choice – this can be on the computer being used to download the files or a USB flash drive. Having done so, you can then install Windows at your leisure, either on the current computer or a different one. All you have to do is click the Setup file.

Windows 10 & Touchscreens

Windows 10 has been designed for use with touchscreens as well as the traditional mouse/keyboard combo. To this end, it comes with a tablet mode that essentially turns a touchscreen equipped computer into a tablet.

By default, tablet mode is switched off. To turn it on, right-click on the Desktop and then click Display Settings. At the right, click tablet mode to access the feature's settings. Under **Make Windows more touch-friendly when using your device as a tablet,** click the switch to **On.** Clicking in the **When I sign in** box, lets you configure Windows to enter tablet mode automatically.

When your computer is in tablet mode, all actions have to be carried out with touchscreen gestures. These are as follows:

Tap

Tapping once on an object opens, selects, or activates the object depending on what type of object it is. This is the same as clicking with a mouse.

Press and Hold

Press your finger down and hold it there for about a second. Typically, this opens a window that displays information about an item or opens a menu specific to the item. This is similar to right-clicking with a mouse.

Pinch and Stretch

Touch the screen or an item with two or more fingers, then move the fingers towards each other (pinching) or away from each other (stretching). These actions will zoom in and zoom out, respectively.

Slide

Sliding or dragging a finger across the screen lets you move through what's on the screen. This is similar to scrolling with a mouse.

Press and Slide

Pressing and sliding simultaneously lets you move a screen item to a different location. This is the same as dragging with a mouse.

Swipe

Swiping an item with a short, quick movement will select an item and will sometimes open a related menu as well.

Swipe From the Edge

Place your finger on the edge of the screen and slide or swipe it inwards without lifting it. This can do a number of things: open a recently used app or see a list of recently used apps, open another app at the same time, reveal commands and options for the current apps, and close an app by dragging it to the bottom of the screen.

CHAPTER 2

Getting Started With Windows 10

In Chapter Two, we see how to get going with Windows 10. We take a look at the main elements of the interface such as the Desktop, Start Menu and Taskbar. We explain how to access, use, and customize them.

We also examine some new features that include Virtual Desktops, the Action Center, Task Switcher and the new personal assistant, Cortana. Learning how to work with tiles and groups is covered as well.

First Start

When Windows 10 starts for the first time, you are taken to the Lock screen. The screen is a security feature designed to prevent malware such as login scripts from taking control of your computer.

Signing In

Click anywhere on the lock screen to access the sign-in screen. Type your password in the box and click the arrow or just tap **Enter** on the keyboard.

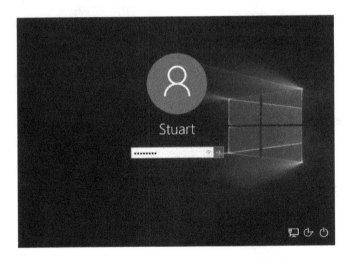

You will see three buttons at the bottom-right of the screen. The first lets you configure your Internet settings if you are not already connected; the second opens a list of accessibility options, such as an on-screen keyboard and Sticky keys; while the third lets you shut the computer down.

The Desktop

After signing in, you are taken to the Desktop. Initially, it is empty apart from the Recycle Bin at the top-left. Running along the bottom of the Desktop is the Taskbar, which we look at on the next page.

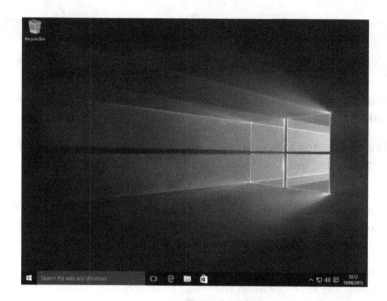

The purpose of the Desktop is to provide an easily accessible location where you can put shortcuts to programs and features you use often. When you open programs or folders, they appear on the Desktop. You can also create folders on the Desktop and use them to categorize and organize your files and programs. To do this, right-click an empty part of the Desktop, and go to **New, Folder**.

On the Desktop, files, folders and programs are represented by icons – double-clicking on an icon will open the item. To place a shortcut to a favorite item on the Desktop, locate the item and then right-click on it. Click **Send to**, and then click **Desktop (create shortcut)**. The shortcut icon appears on your Desktop.

To move an item to the Desktop, browse to where it is located, left-click on it and then just drag it to the Desktop and release it. The position of icons on the Desktop can be arranged in the same way.

Groups of icons can be selected by left-clicking on the screen and dragging to create a box around them. Then you can drag the icons as a group or delete them. Right-clicking on the screen offers a number of other icon-related options as well. These include re-sizing and sorting by various criteria.

To remove an item from the Desktop, right-click on it and then click **Delete**. Note that if the icon is a shortcut, only the shortcut is removed; the original item is not deleted.

The Taskbar

The Taskbar is the long horizontal bar at the bottom of your screen. Unlike the Desktop, which can get obscured by open windows, the Taskbar is almost always visible. It has three main sections:

- The Start button at the far-left, which opens the Start menu

- A middle section, which shows you the programs and files you have open, and allows you to quickly switch between them

- The Notification area at the right, which includes a clock and various icons that indicate the status of certain programs and computer settings

Notification Area
The icons on the notification area indicate the status of open items or provide access to settings. When you mouse over a particular icon, you will see that icon's name or the status of a setting.

For example, the network icon tells you whether or not you are connected to the Internet. The set of icons on the notification area depends on the programs and services on the computer and how it was set up.

Double-clicking an icon usually opens the program or setting associated with it. Occasionally, an icon will display a small pop-up window to notify you about something, such as the successful installation of a new hardware device.

Middle Section
The middle section of the Taskbar enables you to keep track of what's happening on your computer. If you have several items open at the same time, they will often cover each other, or obscure the screen, making it difficult to see what items are underneath or remember what's open.

It does this by showing an icon for each open item.

So if you have four folders open for example, mousing over the folder icon on the Taskbar will reveal thumbnails of all the folders with the names of each one clearly displayed. The contents of each folder can be displayed and they can be closed from their thumbnail. You can also right-click on the folder icon in the Taskbar and close all the folders simultaneously.

Furthermore, the Taskbar displays different icons for different types of item. Have a Notepad note open as well as the folders, and on the Taskbar you'll see both a folder icon and a notepad icon.

This part of the Taskbar also has four default buttons. The Task view 🔲 button opens thumbnails of all running programs; the Microsoft Edge 🅴 button opens the new Edge browser; the File Explorer ▯ button lets you explore your computer; and the Store 🛒 button takes you to the Windows Store.

Moving along to left of the Taskbar we have the search box. This lets you search not only the computer but the Internet as well. When you use it for the first time, Windows 10's personal assistant, Cortana, will spring to life. We take a look at Cortana on pages 31-32. If you don't want a search box on your Desktop, you can get rid of it by right-clicking on the search box and going to **Cortana** and then deselecting **Show search box**.

Other options are available from the right-click menu as well. For example, clicking **Properties** at the bottom of it opens a range of Taskbar options. You can lock it in its current location, move it to the top or either side of the Desktop, make the Taskbar buttons and icons smaller, and even auto-hide it so that it is only visible when you mouse over it.

You will also see a Customize button for the Notification area. Here, you will be able to choose which icons to display, deactivate system icons, disable app notifications, and specify which apps can show notifications.

At the far-left of the Taskbar is the Start menu button. This has one purpose – open the Start menu as we see on the next page.

The Start Menu

The Start menu is the main gateway to your computer's programs, folders, and settings. It's called a menu because it provides a list of choices, just as a restaurant menu does. And as "start" implies, it's often the place that you'll go to start or open things. For example:

- Start programs

- Access commonly used system folders

- Search for files, folders and programs

- Access and adjust your computer's settings

- Turn the computer off

- Log off from Windows or switch to a different user account

To open the Start menu, click the **Start menu** button at the left of the Taskbar or tap the **Windows key** on your keyboard. It will open as shown below:

Start Menu Layout

Starting at the top-left, you'll see your account name (and picture if one is associated with the account). Click on the name to access the settings for the account, to switch to the Lock screen, and to sign out from Windows.

Below, is a list of the programs you use the most. Note that the default programs will soon change as you use the computer.

At the bottom-left, you'll see four links that provide quick access to the most important parts of Windows. **File Explorer** lets you browse the computer's file system to find your data; **Settings** lets you configure just about every aspect of Windows; and **All apps** opens a list of all the programs on the computer – scroll down to see them all.

In the middle of the Start menu are two groups of apps. At the left is **Life at a glance** – a collection of productivity apps that you will mainly use for work and at the right is **Play and explore** – a collection of apps that will mainly be used to keep yourself entertained. Both collections are comprised of "live tiles" that can show updated content.

Customizing the Start Menu

Out of the box, many people are going to find the Start menu is not to their taste. Fortunately, just about every aspect of it can be changed to make it work the way you want it to.

Moving Tiles
One of the first things you will want to do is change the position of some or all of the default tiles. This is very simple to do – just left-click on the tile and then drag it to where you want it to go – when in position, release it. You will find that you can also drag tiles to the Desktop; in this case, though, the tile is not moved, just copied.

Removing Tiles
It's almost a cert that you will find many of the default tiles completely superfluous to your requirements, and that the space they occupy can be put to much better use.

To remove a tile from the Start menu, right-click on it. A menu will open showing several options: Select the top option, **Unpin from Start**. Note that this does not delete the tile's app from the computer, it just removes it from the Start menu.

Adding Tiles
Now that you've created some space on the Start menu, it's time to put something on it that you're actually going to use. You can use the search box on the Taskbar to locate the required apps or click **All apps** on the left of the Start menu. Whichever, having found an app, click on it and drag it to the menu. Note that you can only add tiles – system folders can not be added.

Creating Tile Groups

On pages 22-23, we saw how the Start menu starts you off with two default collections of tiles – **Life at a glance** and **Play and explore**. These tile collections are known as groups and it is very easy to create your own. The ability to do this can be very useful with regard to organizing the Start menu.

Locate the first tile to be placed in your new group and drag it to an empty part of the Start menu. As you do so, you'll notice a blue bar appear; when it has, release the tile. (If you release the tile before the blue bar appears, it will be added to an existing group.)

There will be a gap between the new tile and the one above it. Move your mouse to the gap and a **Name group** link will appear. Click to open it and then type in a name for your group.

In the example above, we have created a new tile group called Favorites.

Virtual Desktops

What is a Virtual Desktop?

If you have a single monitor attached to your computer, you have one screen, i.e. desktop – on which to run all your apps. This is fine for light use, such as switching between a browser and a program such as Microsoft Office. For heavy use though, where you have lots of apps running concurrently, things can quickly get confusing or just plain cumbersome.

This is where virtual desktops come into play. Effectively, they are extra monitors and you can have as many as you need. This enables you to create different workspaces or screens for different applications. For example, you can have your real desktop populated with work apps, and a virtual desktop populated with leisure related apps.

Creating a Virtual Desktop

Go to the Taskbar and click the **Task view** 🔲 button (alternatively, press the Windows and Tab keys simultaneously). This button reveals all the virtual desktops that have been set up. Initially though, there won't be any and all you'll see is a **New desktop** button at the far-right.

Click the **New desktop** button and a virtual desktop is created. Click it again to create a second one, and so on as we see below:

Desktop 1 is the real desktop, the others are all virtual. You will notice that while they look identical to the real desktop, they won't have any programs running on them.

Click on any one of the desktops to go to it. You can switch to any of the others at any time simply by clicking the **Task view** button, which will reveal them all as shown above.

If you have program windows open on a virtual desktop, they show on the thumbnail of the desktop on the Task view interface as we see in the image at the top of the next page.

cont'd

When you move your mouse over a desktop that has programs open on it, those programs are displayed as large thumbnails. Click on one of the thumbnails to make that program (and the corresponding desktop) active.

You can move programs among the different desktops you've set up. To do so, click the **Task view** button to reveal all the desktops, hover the mouse over the desktop containing the program to be moved, and then simply drag it to the required desktop.

Another way is to right-click on the large thumbnail of the program and then select **Move to** and then the required desktop.

To close a desktop, click the **Task view** button on the Taskbar to bring up the Task view interface. Move your mouse over the thumbnail for the desktop you want to close. Click the **X** button that displays in the upper-right corner of the thumbnail.

Action Center

Windows has long had a feature called Notifications that opens an advisory pop-up window on the screen whenever something has happened that it thinks the user should be aware of. A typical example is when a program has automatically updated itself.

The problem with this is that these notifications are easily overlooked, particularly if you are busy with something else. The Action Center in Windows 10 provides the solution. Basically, it provides a way of reviewing your notification history so you can check something you neglected to look at earlier, or indeed if there is anything you have missed completely.

To access the Action Center, tap the ▦ button at the far-right of the Taskbar. You can also open it by pressing the **Windows key + A**.

Notifications are categorized and displayed by type, e.g. Autoplay, Security and Maintenance, etc. Click a notification to open it and activate any actions that need to be carried out.

At the right of many notifications, you'll see a down-arrow – click this to reveal more details. Hover the mouse over the notification to reveal an **X** button – click this to remove the notification from the panel.

At the bottom of the Action Center are "quick action" buttons that provide access to commonly used features, such as Tablet mode, which switches Windows 10 between desktop and tablet modes; and All settings, which provides access to all the computer's settings.

VPN lets you quickly connect or disconnect from a virtual private network; Note lets you quickly create a note in OneNote; Location turns your computer's location-based services on or off; and Quiet hours mutes all the notifications.

If you click the **All settings** button and go to **System > Notifications and actions,** you will see a number of customization options for the Action Center. Amongst other things, you will be able to specify which "quick actions" to show, turn app notifications off, and set notifications to show on the Lock screen.

Keyboard Shortcuts

Windows 10 introduces a number of keyboard shortcuts to help with using its new features, such as virtual desktops and the Cortana personal assistant.

Window Snapping
Window snapping (see pages 43-44) helps the user to arrange open windows on the desktop:

- **Windows key + left arrow** – snap active window to the left of the screen

- **Windows key + right arrow** – snap active window to the right of the screen

- **Windows key + up arrow** – snap active window to the top of the screen

- **Windows key + down arrow** – snap active window to the screen bottom

Virtual Desktops
The Windows key can also be used with the virtual desktops feature:

- **Windows key + Ctrl + D** – create a new virtual desktop

- **Windows key + Ctrl + left arrow** – scroll left through your desktops

- **Windows key + Ctrl + right arrow** – scroll right through your desktops

- **Windows key + Ctrl + F4** – close the current desktop

- **Windows key + Tab** – open the task view that shows all open desktops

Cortana
Keyboard shortcuts for Windows 10's new personal assistant include:

- **Windows key + Q** – opens Cortana ready for voice input

- **Windows key + S** – opens Cortana ready for typed input

Navigation
Windows 10 keyboard shortcuts apart, there are plenty of old classics that have survived successive versions of the operating system and are still going strong:

- **Windows key + ,** – temporarily hide apps to briefly show the desktop

- **Windows key + D** – minimize apps to go straight to the desktop

- **Windows key + Home** – minimize all windows except the one being used

- **Windows key + L** – lock your PC and go to the Lock screen

- **Windows key + E** – launch File Explorer (aka Windows Explorer)

cont'd

- **Windows key + any number key** – opens the app pinned to the Taskbar in the numbered position, e.g. Win + 2 opens the second app on the Taskbar

- **Windows key + T** – cycle through taskbar items (hit Enter to launch)

- **Windows key + R** – opens the Run dialog box

- **Windows key + U** – cycle through taskbar items (hit Enter to launch)

- **Windows key + Space** – switches input language and keyboard

- **Alt + Up arrow** – go up one level in File Explorer

- **Alt + Left arrow** – go to the previous folder in File Explorer

- **Alt + Right arrow** – go to the next folder in File Explorer

- **Alt + Tab** – switch between windows

- **Alt + F4** – close the current window

- **Alt + Right arrow** – go to the next folder in File Explorer

Pictures, Video and Display
Windows 10 is a very visual OS and there are keyboard shortcuts to help you capture screenshots, record on-screen activity and zoom in and out:

- **Windows key + Print Screen** – takes a screenshot and saves it in the Pictures folder

- **Windows key + G** – opens the Game DVR recorder (if supported by your graphics card).

- **Windows key + Alt + G** – start recording activity in the current window

- **Windows key + P** – switches between display modes (with a secondary display connected)

- **Windows key + Plus** – zoom in using the Magnifier utility

- **Windows key + Minus** – zoom out using the Magnifier utility

Task Switcher

Windows 10 gives you several ways to switch between open windows and programs – collectively known as "tasks". Being able to do this is essential for people who want, or need, to work efficiently.

A very useful feature in Windows 10 with regard to this is the way open tasks are highlighted on the Taskbar with an underline as we see here.

This gives you an at-a-glance view of current tasks and gives you a good idea of what's going on, particularly if you recognize the programs from their icons.

The main method of switching between them is the **Alt + Tab** keyboard shortcut, which is known as the Windows task switcher. Press the two keys simultaneously to open the task switcher and you will see large thumbnails of all the open programs as shown below:

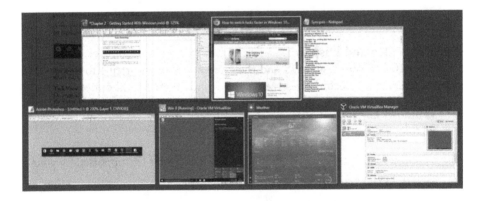

Then, while holding **Alt** down, tap the **Tab** key to flick through the tasks. When you get to the one you want to switch to, release the **Alt** key – it will then open on the Desktop. You will notice that each program has a large text label at the top, which further helps to identify the programs.

It is also possible to close programs from the task switcher. Hover the mouse over the program you want to close and an **X** will appear at the top-right corner – click it to close the program.

The Task view button we discussed on pages 25-26 does the same thing – it shows thumbnails of all open programs and allows you to switch between them using the mouse rather than the **Tab** key.

Cortana

What is Cortana?

Cortana is Microsoft's version of Apple's "Siri" and Google's "Google Now" personal assistants. It will help you find things on your computer, manage your calendar, find files, and even chat with you. Furthermore, Cortana learns as it goes along, so the more you use it, the more personalized your experience with it becomes.

There are two ways to interact with Cortana: by text entry on your keyboard and by voice via a microphone. Your computer may have one built-in but if not, stand microphones are available for less than $10 and headsets with microphones are available for just a little more.

Configuring a Microphone

If you want to operate Cortana by voice, you must first set up the microphone.

1. Click the **Start button** at the bottom-left corner of the screen and then click **Settings, Time & Language**

2. Click **Speech** on the left

3. In the Microphone section, click the **Get started** button

4. In the **Set up your mic** window, click **Next**

5. You will be given a sentence to read aloud. If the microphone picks up your voice the setup is done. Click the **Finish** button

Setting Up Cortana

Before you can use Cortana, it needs some basic configuration. Get started by clicking in the search box to the right of the Start button.

A window will pop up offering a brief overview of what Cortana can do for you. If you are not interested in using the feature, click the **Not interested** button – this lets you stick with the standard Windows search utility. If you do want to use Cortana however, click the **Next** button.

You'll then need to agree to a privacy statement since, in order to work, Cortana needs information about you. This includes your computer's location, your contacts, web history and so on.

Cortana only works with a Microsoft account, as it saves information about you online. So if you're currently using a local Windows account to log in to your computer, you'll be prompted to switch to a Microsoft account by signing into an existing account or by creating a new one.

Personalizing Cortana

Cortana will build up a profile about you as you use it and you can speed up this process by telling it what you're interested in. Click in the search box and click the **Notebook** icon.

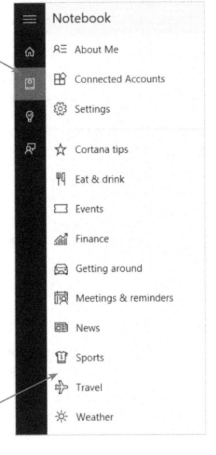

All the information Cortana holds on you is kept in the Notebook. Right at the top of the Notebook is an **About me** link. Click this to edit your name (how Cortana addresses you) and your locations – home, work, etc. Cortana will then be able to give travel directions, traffic updates before you travel and so on.

Below **About me** is a **Settings** link. This lets you configure Cortana in a number of ways. This includes enabling "Hey Cortana", which lets you make a voice query simply by saying Hey Cortana rather than clicking the microphone icon each time

You can also use the Notebook to tell Cortana what your interests are. This is done by opening the various categories and seeing what options are available; these will be different for each category.

The Eat & Drink category, for example, lets you specify your price range, the type of cuisine, and how far you are prepared to travel.

Using Cortana

Once it has been set up, you can query Cortana by text (click in the search box) or by voice (click the microphone button at the right of the search box). Whichever method you use, Cortana will then display a summary of information it thinks you'll be interested in. You'll get this every time you click in the box but, over time as the feature gets to know your interests, this will become more relevant.

Cortana can search your PC for specific files, applications and settings. You can ask it more general questions, and even use it to search the web – just ask it a question, as you would a person. You can also give Cortana commands such as sending an email, or making an appointment for a certain date.

Adding Users

Windows 10 makes it possible for any number of people to use a computer by allowing each person to have their own personal account. Depending on the type of account, they can configure and personalize their accounts by changing the wallpaper and colors, they can install software that's only accessible from their account, and install and set up hardware.

The ability to do this is particularly useful in a home environment where several family members all use the computer. By giving each their own account, which they can customize to suit their specific requirements and tastes, a single computer can be used sensibly and without conflict.

Another useful application of user accounts is to password-protect the main administrator account and then create standard accounts for the kids. They can use the computer but won't be able to compromise its security or performance due to the limitations placed on standard accounts.

Account Types

When Windows 10 is installed, an administrator account is created by default. However, the user also has the option of creating and using a standard account. Lets take a look at both types and see the pros and cons:

- **Administrator Accounts** – the administrator account has complete access to the computer and can make any desired changes. Most people use it simply because it's already there (it's the default account). The drawback is that any program that is run on an administrator account also has complete access to the computer – this is how malware and viruses get on to a user's system

  Administrator accounts come in two types: a Microsoft account, which you have to sign in to with a Microsoft registered email address and password; and a Local account, which just requires a user name and password. The drawback with the latter is that you won't be able to download apps from the Windows Store (although you can browse it) and many Microsoft apps on the computer won't work

- **Standard Accounts** – standard accounts are much safer as they do not allow users to make unauthorized changes that affect the system. If a standard account user tries to install a program for example, they will need to enter a password, i.e. they need permission, before being allowed to.

  However, while they may not be able to install programs, make changes to global settings, etc, they will be able to do just about anything else. Therefore, on a day-to-day basis, being restricted to a standard account will present no problems to the average user.

Creating a New User

Creating an account for another person to use is very easy to do:

1. Click the **Start** button and then click **Settings**

2. Click **Accounts**

3. Click **Family & other users**

4. If the account is for a member of the family, click **Add a family member**

5. Select either **Add a child** or **Add an adult** (the first option sets restrictions on what the child can do on the computer)

6. Enter the new user's email address and click **Next**

7. In the **Add this person?** window, click the **Confirm** button

8. The next window tells you that an invitation has been sent to the user's email address and that they'll need to accept the invitation in order to change settings for their new account. Click **Close.** A standard account is now available for the new user to log in to

Signing in to, or Switching, Accounts

Once a new account has been created, when the computer is started, a login option for the new user will be available on the login screen. Click it, enter the password, and the account will open.

It is also possible to switch to a different account without having to turn the computer off and then back on. To do this, click the Start button to open the Start menu. At the top-left corner of the menu, click the administrator account to reveal a list of all the accounts on the computer. Click the desired account to open the login screen where the account's password will need to be entered.

Changing Account Type

You may, at some point, wish to change an administrator account to a standard account, or vice versa. This is done in Account settings:

1. Click the **Start** button and go to **Settings, Accounts, Family & other users**

2. Click the required account and then click **Change account type**

3. Select **Administrator** or **Standard User** and click **OK**

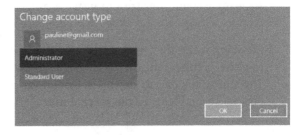

CHAPTER 3

Windows Basics

In this chapter, we take a look at the concept of computer windows. We explain how windows are constructed, and the various elements that go to make up the typical computing window, such as menus and dialog boxes.

We also explain the various ways in which windows can be manipulated such as moving, resizing and arranging. This is essential not only in working with them but also in terms of organization.

Window Structure

Windows are two-dimensional objects arranged on a plane called the Desktop. In a modern full-featured windowing system they can be resized, moved, hidden, restored or closed. Windows usually include other graphical objects, including a menu bar, toolbars, controls, icons and often a working area.

In the image below, which is of the Documents folder in Windows 10, we see a typical window and the elements of which it is comprised:

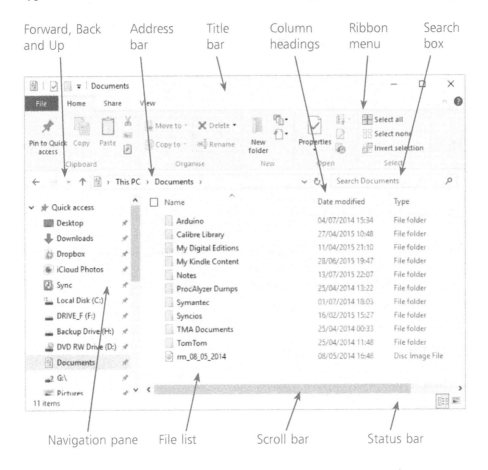

Forward, Back and Up   Address bar   Title bar   Column headings   Ribbon menu   Search box

Navigation pane   File list   Scroll bar   Status bar

The working area of a single window usually holds only one main object. However, secondary "child windows", such as tabs in web browsers, for example, makes it possible to have several similar documents or objects running within a single main window.

Windows can be arranged so that they do not overlap (tiled windows) or so they do overlap (overlaid windows). They can be maximized so they fill the entire screen or minimized so they don't occupy any screen space.

Menus

A menu is a set of options presented to the user of a computer application to assist in finding information or executing a program or function. Menus are common in graphical user interfaces (GUIs) such as Windows or the Mac OS. They are also employed in some speech recognition programs. Menus come in various types that include:

- **Drop-Down Menus** – in this type of menu, clicking an item causes a list of new items to appear below that item. Clicking on one of the items in the list either executes the indicated function or generates a submenu

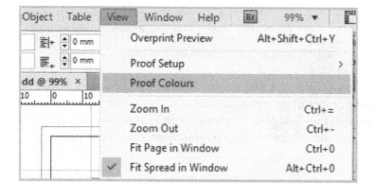

- **Fly-Out Menus** – a variant of the drop-down menus, with fly-out menus the list appears to the side of the clicked item

- **Drop-Line Menus** – with this type of menu, a bar appears below the main menu with menu options as in the example below:

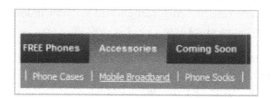

- **Accordion Menus** – when you click the main menu item, the menu expands in a downwards direction. Clicking the main item again causes the menu to retract

- **Split Menus** – this is in two parts so the menu is literally "split". The parent items are in the main position and the child items in the sidebar.

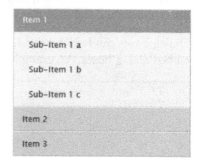

Dialog Boxes

A dialog box is a window that allows users to perform a command, asks users a question, or provides users with information or progress feedback. A typical example is shown below:

Dialog boxes consist of a title bar (to identify the command, feature, or the originating program), an optional main instruction (to explain the user's objective with the dialog box), various controls in the content area (to present options), and commit buttons (to indicate how the user wants to commit to the task).

Dialog boxes come in two fundamental types:

● **Modal dialog boxes** – these temporarily halt the program until the user has responded. Typical scenarios are when the program requires some additional information before it can continue, or when it wishes to confirm that the user wants to proceed with a potentially dangerous course of action

● **Modeless dialog boxes** – this type of dialog box is used when the requested information is not essential to continue, and so the window can be left open while work continues elsewhere

On a similar vein, we have task panes. These are essentially the same as dialog boxes except that they are presented within a window pane instead of a separate window. As a result, task panes have a more direct, contextual feel than dialog boxes.

Dialog boxes can have tabs and, if so, they are called tabbed dialog boxes. An example is shown below:

Minimizing & Maximizing Windows

Minimizing Windows

There are times when you aren't using a window but don't want to shut it down completely. The solution is to minimize the window. This removes it from the screen but doesn't close it.

To do it, just click the – button at the right of the title bar.

This will minimize the window to the Taskbar where you will see its icon is still in place as we see below:

Maximizing Windows

At other times, you will want as much working area as possible. Or, you may need to enlarge a window in order to see all its contents. In both situations, you need to maximize the window.

When you do this, the window will fill the entire screen. Click this button.

Other methods of minimizing, maximizing and restoring are:

- **Minimize** – click the window's icon on the Taskbar

- **Maximize** – double-click the window's title bar

- **Restore** – restore a maximized window to its previous state by double-clicking its title bar. To restore a minimized window, click its icon on the Taskbar

Moving Windows

There will often be occasions when you need to move a window to a different part of the screen – usually this is when you have several windows open at the same time and so need to organize your desktop.

This is the way to do it:

1. First, make sure the window is not maximized, i.e. it isn't occupying the entire screen

2. Position the mouse pointer over the window's title bar but not over the icons at the left and right of the bar

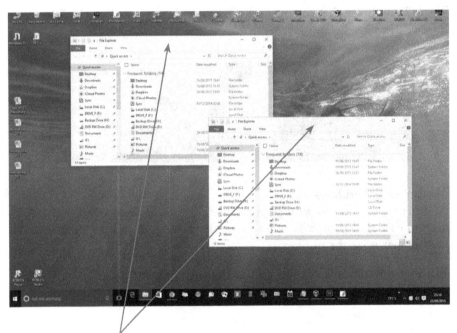

3. Click on the title bar and then keeping the mouse button depressed, drag the window to where you want it to go. You will see the window and its contents move as you drag it along

4. When the window is in the required position, release the mouse button

If you have two monitors connected to your computer thus extending your desktop, you can drag open windows from one desktop to the other as described above.

Resizing Windows

Sometimes you will need more precision than the Maximize and Minimize commands offer. Instead of all or nothing, you'll want something in-between, i.e. a setting of your own choice.

This can be done as follows:

1. If you want to adjust the height of the window, position the pointer on either the top or bottom edge of the window

2. If you want to adjust width of the window, position the pointer on either the left or right side of the window

3. If you want to adjust both height and width simultaneously, position the pointer in any corner of the window

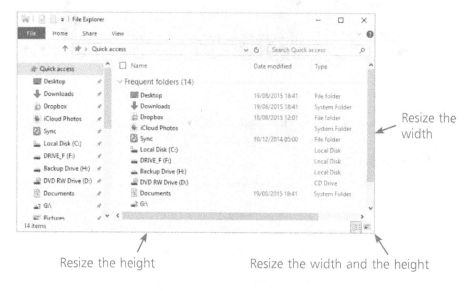

Resize the height   Resize the width and the height

4. When the mouse pointer is correctly positioned, it turns into a two-headed arrow

5. Click the left mouse button and drag the border to resize the window as necessary

6. Release the mouse button to set the border in its new position

7. Repeat the exercise with any other borders that need to be resized.

Remember that you can resize a window both vertically and horizontally at the same time by dragging from a corner.

Arranging Windows

Rather than resize and move your windows manually, you can take advantage of some Windows 10 features that do the job automatically.

The procedure is:

1. Right-click on an empty area of the Taskbar to open a menu containing a list of useful shortcuts as shown below:

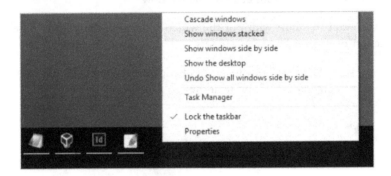

2. Select from the following three options in the menu:

- **Cascade windows** – this automatically arranges all your open windows in an overlapping arrangement that reveals the title bars of each while resizing them equally

- **Show windows stacked** – this resizes the windows equally and arranges them across the screen in rows

- **Show windows side by side** – similar to the **Show windows stacked** option, this arranges the windows in columns

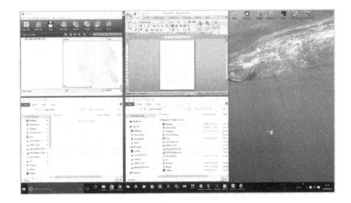

Windows arranged with the side by side option

Snap Assist

Snap Assist is a windows management feature that lets you arrange open windows, including maximizing and resizing, simply by dragging and dropping them to different edges of the screen.

First introduced in Windows 7, the Windows 10 version also lets you snap windows to each corner of the screen. This offers more flexibility when working with multiple applications. The feature works as follows:

Snapping a Window to the Left or Right of the Screen

Position the mouse pointer on the window's title bar. Left-click and drag the window to the left or the right. When the pointer hits the screen's edge, the window snaps to it and also resizes to fill that half of the screen.

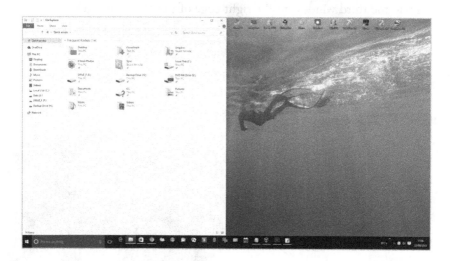

Snapping a Window Vertically

Move the mouse pointer over the window's title bar until you see it turn into a double-headed arrow. Then drag it to the top of the screen – as it hits the screen's edge, the window will maximize vertically.

Restoring a Snapped Window

If you drag a snapped window away from the edge of the screen, it will revert to its original dimensions. It won't put it back in the original position though. To do this, double-click on the window's title bar.

Snapping Multiple Windows

The Snap assist feature has another trick up it sleeve – it lets you snap windows to each corner of the screen. This makes it possible to have the screen completely filled with four equally sized windows. Or, if you prefer, two on one half and one on the other – the permutation is up to you.

Lets say you want an arrangement similar to the one mentioned above – two windows filling the left half of the screen and another filling the right half:

1. Position the mouse pointer on the first window's title bar. Left-click and drag the window to the top-left corner of the screen

2. When you see an outline of the position the window will take appear, release the mouse button. The window will snap into position filling the top-left corner of the screen

3. Following the same procedure, drag the next window to the bottom-left corner. The window will snap into place filling the bottom-left corner

4. Drag the third window to the right edge of the screen and release it

Two windows on the left   One window on the right

Getting windows to snap into the corners of the screen can be a bit awkward to get the hang of initially. The trick is to do it slowly and to move the mouse pointer right into the corner.

Closing Windows

Like most actions in Windows, there are a number of ways to close a window – choose the one most appropriate to the situation.

If you can see the top-right corner of the window, click the **Close** button on the title bar.

Alternatively, you can right-click on the title bar and then from the control menu, click **Close**

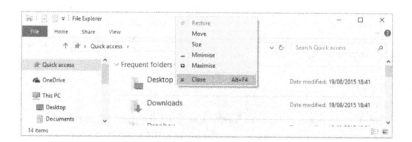

If you can't see the title bar because it is concealed or the window is minimized, locate the window's button on the Taskbar. Move the mouse pointer to the top of the thumbnail and click the **Close** button.

Another way to close a window from the Taskbar is to right-click the window's icon and then click **Close Window** at the bottom of the menu.

Organizing Icons

Every item on your computer is represented by an icon. These let you see the items, open them, close them, select them, etc, etc. The more stuff you have on your computer, the more icons there will be.

Icons you create will be in two places – the Desktop and in folders. Lets see how to organize them in both locations:

The Desktop
We've already seen how desktop icons can be manually moved around the desktop simply by dragging them to the desired position. Windows provides another, automatic, way of arranging them:

1. Right-click on an empty part of the desktop and hold the pointer over **Sort by** to reveal a submenu

2. On the submenu, you will see options to automatically arrange the desktop icons by **Name, Size, Item type** and **Date modified**

3. Hover the mouse over **View** to see another submenu. This lets you set the size of the icons to **Small, Medium** or **Large**. There is also an option to **Auto arrange icons** – if you select this, any new icon created on your desktop will automatically be sorted, based on the current sorting option for desktop icons

Folders
Options for organizing icons in your folders can be accessed by right-clicking in a folder. You will see the same **View** and **Sort by** menu items offering submenus with similar options as for the desktop.

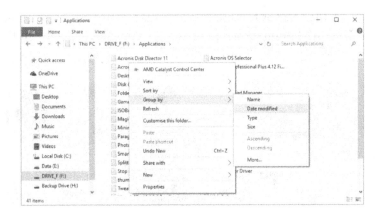

You will also see an option called **Group by**. This lets you automatically organize items in a folder by a wide range of criteria – click the **More** option to see even more options.

CHAPTER 4

File Explorer

File Explorer (formerly known as Windows Explorer), has always been a core element of Windows. Like most of the various sections of the operating system, it's been given a noticeable overhaul in Windows 10.

While the basic layout and functionality will be familiar to anyone who has used Windows XP or later, it has been enhanced with a number of new features. In this chapter, we explain the finer points of the new File Explorer.

We also take a look at some important system folders such as This PC and the Control Panel.

What is File Explorer?

File Explorer, previously known as Windows Explorer, is a file manager application that provides a graphical interface for accessing your computer's file system. The three main ways to access it are:

1. In the Taskbar search box, type **File** and then hit **Enter** on your keyboard

2. If you're on the desktop, click the File Explorer icon on the Taskbar

3. Press the **Windows** key and **E** simultaneously

File Explorer will open as we see below:

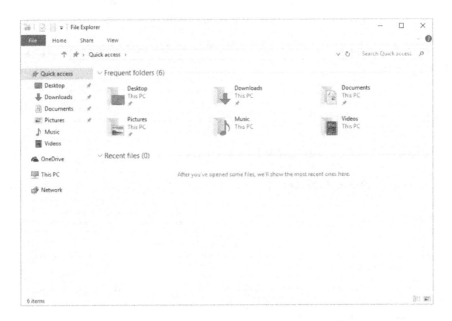

The basic purpose of File Explorer is to provide access to the contents of a given folder. This enables you to work with those contents, whatever they may be. For example, you may want to rename a file, copy it to a different part of the computer, delete it, etc.

File Explorer is designed to help you carry out these actions as easily as possible. Take a look at the address bar – you'll see that it is showing the name of the folder currently being displayed – in this example it is **Quick Access**. This is the folder that File Explorer opens by default and, as the name suggests, it provides access to the folders you use the most. We take a closer look at the Quick Access folder on page 54.

Four folders that will always be present in it are Music, Videos, Documents, and Pictures. These are libraries and we explain their purpose on page 52.

Locating a File

Due to the hierarchical nature of Windows, you will usually have to navigate through a number of folders and subfolders to find the file you want.

Two ways you can do this are:

1. Open File Explorer and take a look at the navigation pane on the left – if you see the folder that contains the required file, all you have to do is click on it. Its contents will appear in the main File Explorer window

2. If the folder you're after is in the main File Explorer area, click it to open it in the same location

However, it's more likely that you won't see the required folder in either of these locations. The reason for this is that files, and the folders that contain them, are almost always in subfolders. To illustrate this, consider the Picture folder on the author's computer:

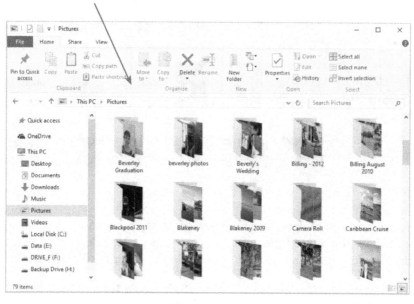

Not a single picture, i.e. file, is to be seen. They are all located in subfolders. To get to a specific file, you have to open the subfolder. You may then find that there are subfolders in the first subfolder – just keep clicking your way through them until you find the required file.

If you don't know the name of the folder that contains the wanted file then things get more difficult. You have two options here: either do a search using the search utility, or use a process of elimination to narrow it down as much as possible. Usually though, particularly if you created the file yourself, you'll have a good idea of where it is.

Exploring With File Explorer

An important part of exploration is keeping track of where you are, and have been – otherwise you may end up getting lost. This is no less true when exploring a computer.

To this end, File Explorer provides the address bar – this shows the address of the currently open folder. As you move from that folder to a subfolder and then to yet another subfolder, the address of each of these folders is added to the address bar. This is demonstrated below:

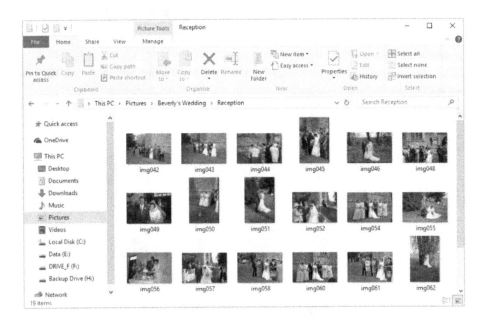

Here, we have had to open four folders to get to the required file. We opened **File Explorer, Pictures** in the default Quick Access folder, **Beverley's Wedding** in the Pictures folder, and finally **Reception** in the Beverley's Wedding folder.

So you can see that the address bar shows quite clearly the route you have taken to get to your current location in Windows.

The address bar can do more though. You can use it to quickly and easily access any of the folders listed in the current address. You have two ways to go:

- **Retrace your steps** – clicking any folder listed in the address bar will take you directly to that folder

- **Go anywhere** – clicking the arrow to the right of any folder in the address bar will open a list of all the subfolders in that folder. This is demonstrated in the image at the top of the next page

cont'd

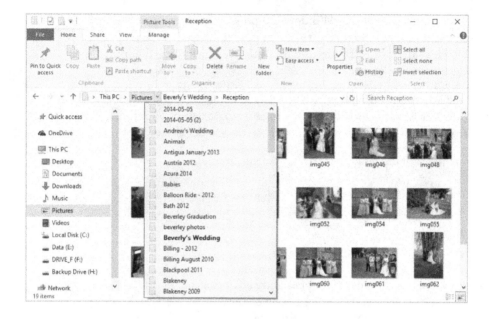

Here, we have clicked the arrow to the right of Pictures – this has opened a list of all the folders in the Pictures folder. To go to any of these folders, just click on it.

Other navigational aids offered by File Explorer include:

- **Back button** – at the left of the address bar you will see a backward pointing arrow. Tap this to go back to the most recently opened folder

- **Forward button** – if you have already opened a subfolder, you can go back to it by clicking the forward arrow which will now be active

- **Recent folders button** – next to the forward button is a down-arrow. Click this to open a list of recently opened folders as shown on the right

- **Up button** – next to the Recent folders button is an up-arrow. Click this to go back to the previous folder

Libraries

The Libraries feature in Windows 10 provides a central place to manage files that are scattered throughout your computer. Instead of clicking through a bunch of directories to find the files you need, including them in a library makes for quicker access.

The important thing to remember is that libraries simply gather files from different locations and display them as a single collection – they are not moved from their location. Essentially, a library is a folder full of shortcuts.

Windows starts you off with four default libraries:

- Music
- Pictures
- Videos
- Documents

As you create files of these types and click **Save As..** on the File menu, you will see the option to save the file to one of the above mentioned libraries. These will be listed right at the top of the navigation pane for easy access.

You are under no obligation to use the Libraries feature but two very good reasons to do so include:

- Your documents and files will always be easy to find

- The libraries are very easy to access. Wherever you are in Windows, just click the File Explorer icon on the Taskbar and your libraries will be available in the Quick Access folder

Creating Libraries
There are several ways to create a new library – the one we explain here is as good as any:

1. Right-click on a folder you want to put in the library

2. Click **Include in library** and then **Create new library**

3. A new library is created and the folder is included in it. The library will be given the same name as the folder

To include another folder in the library, right-click on it and click **Include in library**. You'll see a list of all the libraries, including any you have created yourself. Click the appropriate library and the folder will be added to it.

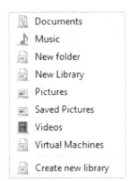

Quick Access

We've already mentioned Quick Access, which you are taken to by default when you open File Explorer. The purpose of this feature is to provide quick access to the folders you use the most.

Initially, it will just show six folders: Desktop, Downloads, and the four libraries. As you use the computer though, and Windows 10 learns your computing habits, it will show other folders as well. These will be the ones that you use the most.

To use the Quick Access folder:

1.   At the top of the navigation pane, you will see the Quick Access button

2.   Click the button, and in main window at the right, your most frequently used folders and most recently used files are displayed as we see below:

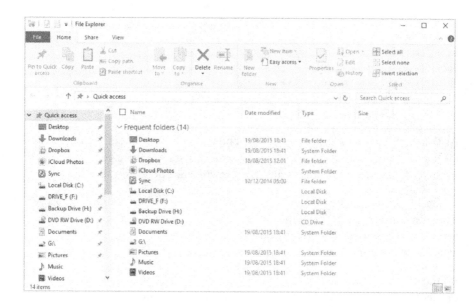

If you look at the navigation pane, your frequently used folders are listed there as well. These folders are all added automatically by Windows and you have no control over which are added and which aren't.

However, you can add folders to Quick Access manually. To do this, right-click on the folder and click **Pin to Quick Access**.

Now open File Explorer and you will see the folder both in the navigation pane at the left and in the main folder at the right.

This PC

A very good way of seeing what's on your computer is to take a look at the This PC folder. To open it, click File Explorer on the Taskbar and then select This PC from the navigation pane. You can also just type **This PC** into the Taskbar search box and hit **Enter**.

At the top of the window, you'll see a ribbon toolbar that offers a number of tools and controls related to drives, networks and system management. Below, are links to the default libraries and the Downloads and Desktop folders.

In the Devices and drives section, you will see all the drives connected to your machine. For users who have more than one hard drive, this is an important feature as it not only lets them access the drives, it provides an at-a-glance view of much storage space each drive has available.

At the bottom of the folder are details of any networks the computer is connected to. At the left-hand side is the navigation pane that provides quick access to other parts of Windows. At the top-right is a search box.

The This PC folder is also very important as it provides access to devices such as digital cameras, smartphones, USB flash drives, etc. When these are connected to the computer, an identifying icon will appear in the Devices and drives section. In the image above, you can see the author's iPhone. To open these devices just click on the relevant icon. You will then be able to access the device's storage area and transfer files to and from the computer.

Those of you who would rather File Explorer open This PC rather than Quick Access, should open File Explorer, click the **View** tab and select **Options**. On the General tab, change the value for **Open File Explorer** to **This PC**.

Drives & Drive Folders

Windows itself, all the files you create, and all the programs you install on the computer, don't live in the ether – all this stuff is kept in a physical location known as a drive.

Most drives these days are solid-state devices and are either installed inside the computer (as with a computer bought from a store) or are connected to a port on the computer's casing. The latter are known as external drives and are often connected to a computer to either extend the amount of storage space available or as a backup device on which to keep data that is too important to lose.

At the top of the list of drives (assuming there is more than one), you'll see one labeled **Local Disk (C:)**. This is the system drive. i.e. the one that Windows is installed on and you'll notice that it has a slightly different icon (a blue window above the drive).

Everything that happens on the computer is actually happening on this drive. It contains all your programs and files and, if it were to fail, you would be quite likely to lose it all – one very good reason to always have an up-to-date backup.

Browsing one of these drives to see what's on it is much the same as browsing Windows itself – these devices use the same hierarchical file structure. To open a drive, click its icon in the This PC folder:

Above, we see the author's backup drive, which is an external USB drive connected to the rear of the computer. It opens in the This PC view as shown above and can be used in exactly the same way as the Windows drive.

Control Panel

The Control Panel is a system folder which allows you to view and manipulate basic system settings and controls. For example: adding hardware, adding and removing software, controlling user accounts, and changing accessibility options. Additional controls (known as applets) can be provided by third party software.

To open the Control Panel, right-click on the **Start** button and click **Control Panel**. It will open in the "Category" view:

Click a category to see what tools and controls are available. Alternatively, click the **View by:** button and select **Small icons** or **Large icons** to see all the tools.

We won't go into the various options but they will enable you to configure every single part of your system. We recommend that you take a good look at what's available here and guarantee that you will discover an aspect of Windows that you never knew existed.

Should you find something that you are likely to make use of, you can always create a shortcut to it by right-clicking and selecting either **Pin to Quick access** or **Pin to Start**.

CHAPTER 5

Working With Files & Folders

In Chapter 5, we see how to work with files and folders. You'll learn how to create, copy, move, name and rename, delete, and search for files and folders. To do all this, Windows provides a number of tools which we will look at.

Increasingly, computing devices are linked to the online world and a computer running Windows 10 is no different. We see how to manage your data with Microsoft's online storage facility, OneDrive.

Creating Files & Folders

Most files are created with a particular program. To do it, click **File** (usually at the top-left of the window) and then click New. To save a file, click the program's **Save As...** command, which is also available from the File menu.

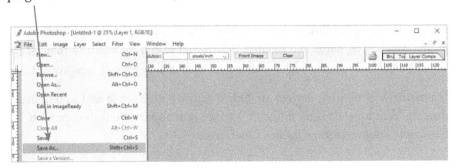

It is also possible to create certain types of file with File Explorer. To do this, open the folder you want to save the file in and then right-click inside the folder. Go to **New** and you will see a menu offering a number of options:

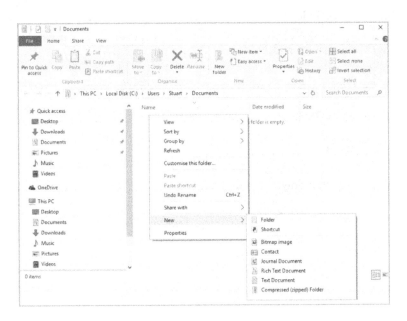

With regard to files, these include a Shortcut (a pointer to an item on the PC), Bitmap image, a Contact to whom you can send email, a Journal document (used with digital pens), a Rich Text Document (a type of Wordpad file), and a Text Document (a plain text file as created with the Notepad program).

You will also see options for creating an empty folder and a compressed folder (see page 64). Folders can be created on the desktop in the same way.

Naming & Renaming a File or Folder

Naming a File or Folder

Having created a file or folder as described on the previous page, you will now want to give it an identifying name. This is very easy to do. For example, when you click **New > Folder** to create a folder, you will see the following:

Click in the box, delete **New folder** and type in the desired name. Windows supports file names up to 255 characters so you can give it an interesting name if you want to.

You will have to name a file when it is created in a program. When you click the **File, New** command you will be prompted to give the file a name.

Renaming a File or Folder

If you don't like the name of a file or folder for some reason, there are several ways to change it to something more to your liking:

- Right-click on the file or folder and click **Rename**. Then enter the new name in the box

- Select the file or folder (see the next page) in File Explorer and then click **Rename** on the ribbon toolbar at the top of the window

- Select the file or folder and then press the **F2** key. The Rename box will appear – delete the old name and enter the new one

Windows will accept most keyboard characters, spaces included. However, it will not accept any names that include * | \ : < > ? /.

Selecting Files & Folders

To be able to work with files and folders, i.e. move them around and all the other things that are possible, you need to be able to select them. This can be done as follows:

1. Open the folder that contains the required file or folder

2. Click on the item's icon – the line it is on will be highlighted in blue

You can then carry out whatever action you want with the file or folder. However, while this will be OK for dealing with a single file or folder, it won't be so clever when you have a whole bunch of them to handle.

A typical example is when you have a number of pictures that you want to download from your digital camera to the computer – moving these one by one will be a slow and tedious procedure. A much better way is to move them all at the same time.

To do this, you need to select all the files as a group. Having done so, you can download them with one command. There are actually several ways to select items as a group. These include:

-   **Selecting consecutive items** – in a folder where all the files are listed consecutively, select the first one by clicking it, then press the **Shift** key and, with it held down, go to the last file in the folder and select it. Now release the **Shift** key. All the files in between the first and last will now be selected

-   **Selecting nonconsecutive items** – in the opposite scenario where the files are not listed in any sort of order you need to do it a different way. Select the first file, press and hold the **Ctrl** key, and then click all the other files. Finally, release the **Ctrl** key – all the files will be selected

-   **Select all command** – make sure the ribbon toolbar at the top of the folder is open and then click **Select all** at the right of the toolbar

-   **Box them in** – with the left mouse button depressed, drag a rectangle around the files you want to select

Having selected some files, you can deselect them if necessary by simply clicking in an empty part of the folder.

Copying/Moving Files and Folders

There are many reasons why you may want to copy or move a file or folder to a different location. With regard to copying, one obvious example is to create a backup copy of an important file.

As with so many Windows actions, there are various ways to do this. One method is to open the folder containing the file to be moved and position it next to the folder the file is to be moved to:

With both folders open, left-click on the file and simply drag it across to the destination folder. When you see **Move to xxx folder** appear below the file, release it – it will now be in the destination folder.

The same method can be used to copy a file as well. In this case, you need to right-click on the file and drag it across. When you release it, a menu will appear offering **Move here, Copy here** and **Create shortcuts here** options. Click the **Copy** option to copy the file across.

When it is not convenient to have the folders arranged alongside each other, you can use the ribbon toolbar. Open the folder containing the file to be moved and select it. On the toolbar, click either the **Move to** or **Copy to** button. A menu of commonly used folders, such as the Desktop, Music, and Pictures will open. Alternatively, you can click **Choose location** and browse to the required destination folder.

Click the required folder and the file will be moved/copied to it.

Previewing Files

The procedure for seeing what's in a file is to double-click on the file's icon, which opens the file in the program that was used to create it. If you don't want the bother of doing this though and just need a quick glance at the file, Windows provides the answer in the form of it's File preview feature.

Preview a file as follows:

1. Open File Explorer

2. Click the **View** tab

3. Click **Preview pane**

4. Browse to the file you want to preview and select it

5. A preview of the file appears in the Preview pane at the right side of the window

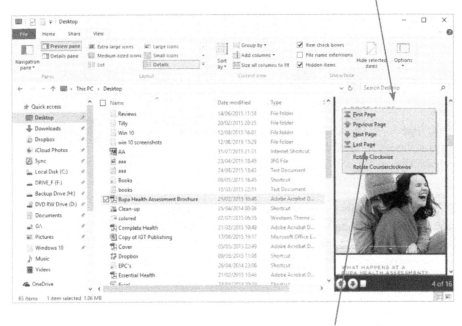

6. Right-clicking on the preview may reveal some options depending on the type of the file. The file shown above is a PDF file that has several pages, so the right-click menu offers First, Previous, Next and Last page options

Note that not all types of file are supported by the Preview feature. In this case, nothing will appear in the Preview pane.

Deleting Files & Folders

Given the enormous capacities of current drives, lack of storage space is much less of an issue than it used to be. That said, you can still find yourself running out of space, particularly if you keep a lot of image and video files on the computer. Another issue that can result from too much clutter is that of performance – the more stuff on your computer, the slower it will run. You may also get spurious errors, reboots and other problems.

So while you may have plenty of space on your drive, it is still a good idea to get rid of stuff you don't need. Deleting files is easy enough to do – just right-click on the file and click the **Delete** button. If you have a bunch of files that need showing the door, select them as a group as we described on page 60 before clicking **Delete**.

However, you should know that files deleted in this way are not actually deleted – they are placed in a system folder called the Recycle Bin. You'll find this folder on the desktop. The purpose of the Recycle Bin is to give you a chance to get a file back if you change your mind or if you deleted it accidentally.

Should you wish to recover a file, open the Recycle Bin, right-click on the file and click **Restore** – it will be moved back to its original location. Another way, assuming it has just been deleted, is to press **Ctrl + Z**. You will also see options on the ribbon toolbar that let you restore files.

When you are sure that a particular file, or bunch of files, really has to go, the following actions will remove it from the computer completely.

- Open the Recycle Bin, right-click on the file and select **Delete**

- To delete all the files in the Recycle Bin in one go, right-click on the Recycle Bin icon and click **Empty Recycle Bin** – everything will go

- On the ribbon toolbar, click **Empty Recycle Bin**

A more drastic method of file deletion involves a procedure known as "formatting". This is carried out on a drive and it basically deletes the existing file system on the drive and replaces it with a new one. The process also wipes the drive clean of all data.

To do it, open the **This PC** folder and right-click on the drive. From the menu that appears, click **Format...** After a moment a window will appear offering various formatting options. Click the **Start** button at the bottom.

Note that the C: drive on which Windows is installed cannot be formatted for obvious reasons. All other drives can be though.

Compressed Folders

File compression is a process of "packaging" a file (or files) to reduce its size. It works by minimizing redundancy in the file's code. Compression software makes it possible to take many files and compress them into a single file, which is smaller than the combined size of the originals.

Most of the files you download form the Internet, such as apps and email attachments, arrive on your computer in a compressed state. Windows computers have a built-in file compression system that compresses and decompresses these files automatically without the user ever knowing about it.

However, file compression is also available for the user. For example, you may want to reduce the size of a folder containing pictures. Or, you can compress the contents of an entire drive in order to gain some storage space. There are two ways to do it:

1. Right-click on the folder or drive that you want to compress

2. At the bottom of the menu, click **Properties**

3. On the General tab, click the **Advanced** button

4. Check the **Compress contents to save disk space** box

If you decide to compress a drive, be aware that depending on the size of the drive, the procedure can take hours. Also, if any files or programs on the drive are open, they will bring the compression procedure to a halt.

The second way is to create what's known as a zipped folder – this is another type of compression technique available to Windows users. When a file is placed inside a zip folder, it is automatically compressed. This is the technique to use when you want to compress something to send by email.

1. Right-click on an empty part of the desktop or an open folder

2. At the bottom of the menu, select **New > Compressed (zipped) Folder**

A new zip folder is created. Any file you place inside it will be compressed automatically.

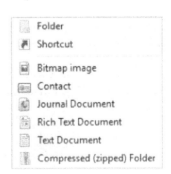

Searching With Windows

The typical computer is literally stuffed to the gills with thousands upon thousands of files. Finding something specific would be a very difficult, if not impossible, task were it not for the search facilities built in to Windows.

When doing a search, you basically have two ways to go:

Computer-wide Searches

If you have no idea of where a particular file, application or setting is located, then you need to use the search box on the Taskbar. Click in the box and just type your query – as you type, results will appear above.

When you look at them, you'll see that they are not taken just from the computer – the feature searches the Windows Store and the Internet as well.

So you will probably need to click the **My stuff** button at the left of the search box. Doing so will eliminate any results taken from the Internet and the Windows Store, and will almost always result in a more manageable and relevant list of suggestions.

Folder Searches

If you know a file is in a particular folder but can't be bothered to search through it, just type your search term in the search box that is at the top-right of every File Explorer window:

The results will appear in the main body of the window – just click one to open it. You will find that many programs offer a search facility as well.

Burning to Disc

Writing, or burning, files to a disc used to be a somewhat complicated procedure thanks to the proliferation of types of disk (CD, CD-R, CD-RW, and DVD).

Windows 8 however, and now Windows 10, has made the process much simpler. In fact, it is no different now than saving a file on any other type of file-storage medium, such as a hard drive or flash drive.

1. Place the disc into the CD/DVD drive

2. Windows will take a few moments to examine the disc

3. Open **This PC** and look for the drive's icon – it will be showing the type of disc, its capacity, and the amount of free space on the disc

4. Click the drive's icon to open the **Burn a Disc** screen

5. We suggest you select the first option **Like a USB flash drive**. This will let you use the disc in exactly the same way as you would a hard drive – saving, deleting, editing, etc

6. Windows will now format the disc to create a file system on it

When the format procedure is done, you can use the disc. Files can be added to it in two ways:

1. Click the drive's icon in This PC to open the disc. Now just drag the files you want to burn on to the window and release them

2. Open File Explorer and browse to the required file. Click the **Share** tab and then click **Burn to disc**

3. A window will open showing the progress of the file transfer. When completed, click the drive to open the disc and see the files on it

Folder Options

By default, folders are presented in a certain way when opened. For example, the ribbon toolbar is minimized. However , you have quite a few options with regard to changing how your folders look and operate.

1. Your first move is to maximize the ribbon toolbar by clicking the little arrow at the top-right corner just below the X button

2. Open the View tab to reveal the available options as we see below:

We won't go into all the ribbon toolbar settings but they make it possible to customize your folders in numerous ways. You can close the navigation pane, activate preview and details panes, alter the size of item icons, and sort your files in a number of ways.

You can also add columns that provide more information with regard to the files, activate check boxes that make it easier to select files, and configure items to show their file type next to their name.

Click the **Options** button at the far-right and a Folder Options window will open as shown on the right.

This offers even more configuration options. For example, you can set File Explorer to open at This PC rather than Quick Access.

It is also possible to set folders to open in their own window.

You can set the mouse to open items with a single click rather than a double click.

At the bottom are some Privacy options, e.g. you can clear File Explorer's history.

OneDrive

The Internet is now ubiquitous in many people's lives so it's no surprise to find that Windows 10 is in on the act as well. It is actually, to a large degree, built around the online world. This is the reason you are urged at almost every turn while using Windows 10 to sign up for a Microsoft account if you haven't already got one.

Having a Microsoft account allows you and Windows 10 to use various online services; one of which is the ability to synchronize your computer's settings with other devices that are linked to that account.

Another benefit is that you can make use of Microsoft's online file storage facility, OneDrive. This is basically a free online drive on which you can store whatever type of files and data you wish. You are given 15GB of space, which is an ample amount in which to store important documents.

Setting Up OneDrive

Click the **Start** button to open the Start menu. Click **All apps** at the bottom-left of the menu and then scroll down to, and click, **OneDrive**.

1. The **Welcome to OneDrive** screen will open. Click the **Get started** button

2. The next window asks you to sign in to your Microsoft account

3. You are introduced to your OneDrive folder. At the bottom of the screen you will see the folder's location on the computer.

    If you want to use a different folder, click the **Change** button and browse to and select the required folder

4. The next window shows you a list of system folders whose contents will be synced (copied) to OneDrive. Next to each is a checkbox that lets you deselect the folder if you don't wish it's contents synced.

When you are happy, click Next. OneDrive is now set up on your PC.

Using OneDrive

The OneDrive feature keeps all its data in one folder, called, not surprisingly, OneDrive. Access it as follows:

1. Click the **Start** button to open the Start menu. Click **All apps** at the bottom-left of the menu and then scroll down to, and click, **OneDrive**

2. Another way is to open File Explorer and look at the navigation pane. Below Quick Access, you'll see OneDrive – click to open it. Its contents, which initially will be just be the default system folders, will be displayed in the main window on the right. Should you wish to do so, you can add more folders – you aren't restricted to the default ones

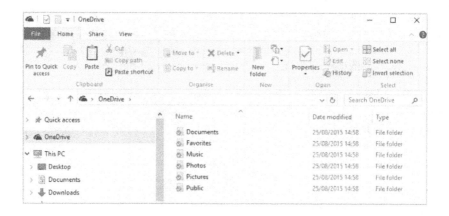

You are now ready to start using OneDrive by adding files to be stored and synchronized online. Proceed as follows:

1. With the OneDrive folder open as above, drag your files from their current folder and drop them in either the OneDrive folder itself or one of the subfolders

2. Alternatively, having created the file, go to **Save as...** on the menu, browse to the OneDrive folder and save it there

Using OneDrive Online

As OneDrive is an online service, it can be accessed via your web browser as well as your computer. To do this:

1. Go to **www.onedrive.live.com** and sign in to your Microsoft account. You will then be able to access OneDrive

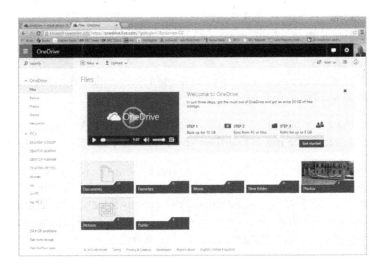

2. You'll be able to use the online version in much the same way as on your computer – creating new files and folders, moving, copying, deleting and more. All changes you make will be replicated on your computer

OneDrive Settings

OneDrive's settings are tucked away in Windows. To access them, click **Settings** in the Start menu and then **System**.

Click **Notifications & actions** and then click **Select which icons appear on the taskbar**. Next to **Microsoft OneDrive**, drag the switch to **On**.

Now look on the taskbar for the OneDrive  icon. Right-click on it and select **Settings**.

CHAPTER 6

Windows 10 Apps

The term "App" is short for application and has replaced the more traditional "computer program".

Windows 10 comes with a number of pre-installed apps, which cover the main functions computers are used for. You will, however, almost certainly want to install your own apps at some point. These can be downloaded from the Windows Store as we'll see.

We show you how to find, download and install apps from the Store, and how to manage and organize them.

Apps and Programs

As we mentioned in the introduction to this chapter, the term "App" is a relatively new one and has largely, but not completely, replaced "program". Its origins are in the world of smartphones and tablet computers, and it refers to the small and basic applications that are used on these devices.

However, Microsoft has seen fit to label all the programs they supply with Windows as apps, so apps they will be! They also offer a lot more apps in the Windows Store.

There are also literally thousands of traditional programs out there. Just so there's no confusion, we'll explain the differences between Windows apps and the older type of program:

Windows Apps
Windows 10, and its predecessor Windows 8, come with a number of built-in apps that cover the main functions of computers. To see a complete list of these apps in Windows 10, open the Start menu, click the **All apps** button and scroll down. You will also see some of them on the right-hand side of the Start menu.

When you click them, they open in a minimalist window that is totally unlike that of traditional computer programs. The apps are easily recognizable by their brightly colored tile-like appearance.

Programs
Traditional computer programs are identifiable by their icons, rather than a large colored tile as with apps.

Also, when you run them, the window they run in will be much more involved and busy in terms of menus, toolbars, and graphics.

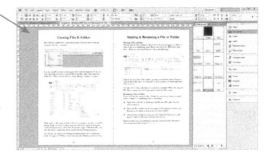

Pre-installed Windows 10 Apps

Much of what the average user does on his/her computer will be covered by the apps supplied with Windows 10. They include:

Alarms & Clock
A simple, yet nevertheless very useful, app that provides four functions: an alarm, a world clock, a timer and a stopwatch. Just type in a location and the world clock feature will tell you the local time.

Calculator
The calculator app can calculate a wide range of data. It offers standard and scientific functions, and conversions that include energy programming, volume, length, weight and mass, and temperature.

Calendar
The calendar is a fairly standard affair that offers Day, Work week, Week, Month and Today views. The calendar's settings let you change the colors, first day of the week, and the days in the work week.

Camera
Intended for people with a Windows 10 smartphone or tablet, the Camera app has a number of useful features, including 4K video recording, auto-HDR, Rich Capture, and a Dynamic Flash mode.

Cortana
Cortana is Windows 10's personal assistant. It will find things on your PC, manage your calendar, find files, and more. The more you use Cortana, the more personalized your experience with it will be.

Food & Drink
The Food & Drink app lets you create and store recipes, create ingredient shopping lists, includes a meal planner, and offers recipes from well known chefs.

Groove Music
For music aficionados, the Groove Music app lets you organize your music collection by album, artist and song. You can create playlists, buy music, and add your music to OneDrive to play anywhere.

Health & Fitness
Health & Fitness provides you with a number of health related options. These include monitoring your diet, fitness workouts, a symptom checker, and conditions look-up.

Maps

This useful app opens showing your current location. With it, you can view maps from literally every part of the globe. You can get directions, find hotels, and get 3D views of famous cities.

Microsoft Edge

The default web browser in Windows 10, Edge replaces the now defunct Windows Explorer. Slick & fast, this new browser does everything that Windows Explorer did and more.

Money

Location-based, the Money app provides real-time information that lets you keep on top of your financial affairs. Keep an eye on global stock markets, create watchlists, convert currencies and much more.

Movies & TV

A simple app that lets you manage all the video content on your computer. This includes home videos, plus TV shows and movies downloaded from the Windows Store. You can also buy from here.

News

Another real-time app, the News app keeps you abreast of what's going on, not just in your part of the world, but globally. Topics covered include sport, trending, entertainment, money, and fitness.

OneDrive

The OneDrive app opens your free online storage. With it, you can store, sync and share data with other people. Files on OneDrive can be accessed directly from a web browser or from your computer.

OneNote

This a note taking application and is part of the Microsoft Office Suite. With it, you can create notebooks, insert pictures, tables, and draw. Your notes can also be saved on OneDrive.

People

A very straightforward app, People is your personal address book. In it, you can keep the contact details, including addresses, phone numbers, and email addresses, of the people in your life.

Photos

Also simple and straightforward, the Photos app is for viewing your pictures. You can use it to organize them in collections and albums, view in a slideshow, enhance, edit and print.

Phone Companion

This app enables you to connect your smartphone (Windows, iOS or Android) to your computer and transfer content between the two. It will also enable you to access music stored on your OneDrive account

Reader

The purpose of the Reader app is to enable you to read different types of document on the computer. This includes file formats such as PDF and TIFF. Documents can also be printed from Reader.

Reading List

As the name suggests, this app lets you create lists of reading material for later perusal. Articles can be taken from the Internet or from other applications on your computer.

Settings

If you need to change any of your computer's default settings, the Settings app is the place to go. With it, you can configure a range of settings including System, Devices, Network, and Security.

Sport

A real-time information app, Sport can keep you updated on literally any sport in the world. Team news, results, fixtures, stories of interest, press reports, league tables – the Sports app has it all.

Store

Store takes you to Microsoft's Windows Store. Here, you will be to browse through literally thousands of apps across all genres, and buy any that will be useful. Some apps can be downloaded for free.

Voice Recorder

The Voice Recorder is an app you can use to record audio. You can use it alongside other apps, which allows you to record sound while you continue working on your computer.

Weather

This provides up-to-date weather forecasts for literally anywhere in the world. It also provides historical weather, shows weather patterns and trends, and the latest weather news from around the world.

Xbox

Xbox connects you to the world of online gaming. Stream your Xbox games to any Windows 10 computer and play new games optimized specifically for Windows 10.

Working With Windows 10 Apps

In Window 8, there was a lot of controversy over the way the default apps looked and operated. When you opened one, you were immediately switched to the Start screen – this made it difficult to use them alongside traditional desktop programs. Not only that, they insisted on taking up the entire screen.

For these reasons, and others, Windows 8 and 8.1 were not popular. With Windows 10, it seems that Microsoft has taken heed of the criticisms (or declining sales!) and come up with a more sensible approach.

For starters, Windows 10 apps now open directly on the desktop. Furthermore, they open in a traditional style window that can be moved and resized.

To move a Windows 10 app around the screen, click on the title bar and then drag to the new location

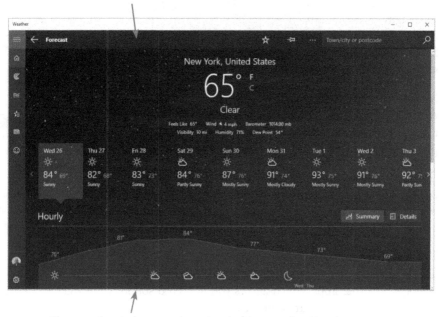

The apps's window can be extended in any direction by dragging the appropriate border. You can resize it vertically and horizontally at the same time by dragging the corners

Toolbars and Menus
Just as with a traditional app, right-clicking on the title bar opens a menu offering Restore, Move, Size, Minimize, Maximize and Close options. These provide you with another way of manipulating your apps.

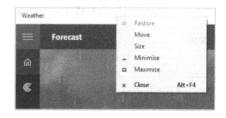

Unlike traditional programs that always almost have a visible toolbar at the top of the screen from where all the program's options and features can be accessed, Windows 10 apps are more discreet.

Take the Groove Music app (shown below) as a typical example:

As with many of the apps, when opened, Groove Music presents a narrow toolbar down the left-hand side. If you click the ☰ icon at the top, the toolbar expands to show the text labels for the various buttons.

As you move about in apps, you will notice an arrow ← button appear at the top-left corner – click it to go back to the previous page. Also on the toolbar, will be a Settings ⚙ button; click it to access the app's settings screen.

With other app's, such as Health & Fitness, right-clicking on the window will open a toolbar of options.

Accessing & Opening Apps

In Windows 10, all apps installed on the computer can be accessed by clicking the **Start menu** button at the left of the taskbar.

When the Start menu opens, click the **All apps** button at the bottom of the screen. You will now see an alphabetical list of all the apps installed on the PC.

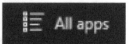

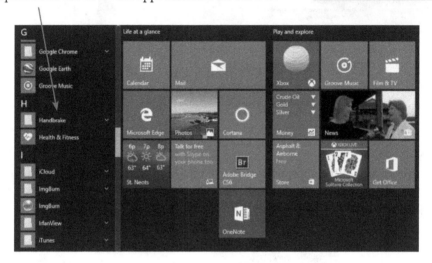

These include the new Windows 10 apps and any traditional apps that have been installed. To open one, just double-click on its icon – its window will open on the Desktop as with the Wordpad example shown below:

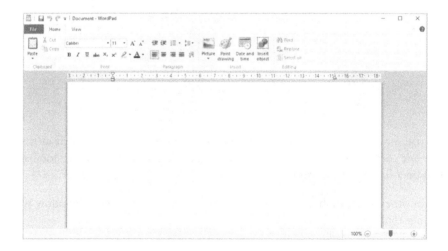

Viewing All Your Apps

As explained on the previous page, the Start menu lists the applications installed on your computer. The scroll menu on the left shows the entire list while the tiles on the right show the ones you use the most, or have pinned there yourself (see page 81 for how to pin apps). On the scroll menu, traditional programs may just show a folder rather than the program itself. In this case, you will see a down-arrow to the right of its folder.

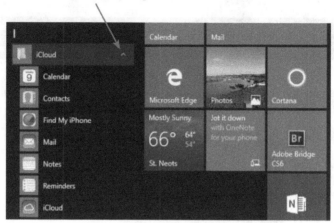

Click the folder and you will see the program's launching icon. You may see other applications related to the main program as well, as we see in the iCloud folder above.

Another way of viewing apps in the Start menu is to click on a letter heading. This opens an alphabetical grid – click on a letter to go to the apps listed under the letter.

Click the **clock** icon at the front of the grid to revert to the beginning of the list and the **globe** icon at the end to go to the end of the list.

Finding Apps

With a brand new computer that has nothing on it but the pre-installed Windows 10 apps, locating those apps won't present much of a challenge. A few months down the line though, when you have installed a load more apps, it might well be a different matter.

This will be the time to start using the search box at the left of the Taskbar:

As soon as you start typing, the search utility will offer suggestions that are based on the letters typed. These will appear in a list above the search box:

By default, the search will include stuff on the Internet. This won't be relevant so click **My stuff** just above the search box to limit the results to apps that are actually on the computer.

Pinning Apps

Windows 10 starts you off with some default apps placed at the right of the Start menu where they can be quickly and easily accessed. You will also see three apps on the Taskbar at the right of the search box.

Should you want to do so, you can add your own apps, or replace the default ones, in both locations. The procedure is known as Pinning. The apps you pin to the Start menu should be ones you use frequently.

Do it as described below:

1. Click the **Start button** to open the Start menu and then click **All apps**

2. Right-click on the app to be pinned

3. To pin the app to the Start menu, click **Pin to Start**

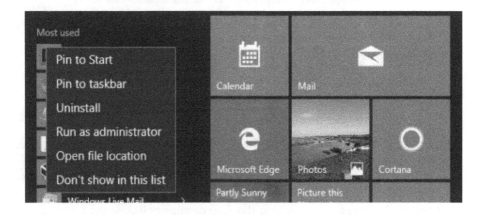

4. To pin the app to the Taskbar, click **Pin to taskbar**

Apps that are open and thus on the Taskbar can also be pinned there. To do this, right-click on the app's taskbar icon and then click **Pin this program to taskbar**.

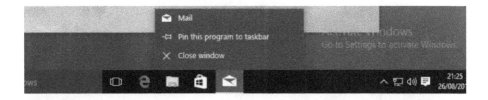

Should you decide to unpin an app from either the Start menu or Taskbar, right-click on it and then click **Unpin from Start** or **Unpin this program from taskbar** respectively.

The Windows Store

When you want to add more functionality to your computer, the Windows Store is the place to go. Here, you will find not just apps but also games, movies and TV shows, and music. We'll concentrate on the apps for now.

To open the Store, click the **Store** icon on the Taskbar. On the opening screen, click **Apps** on the bar at the top of the window:

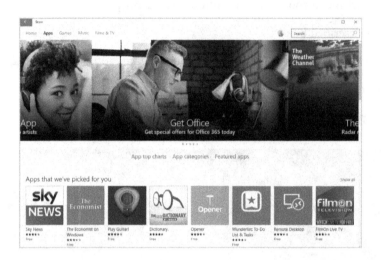

Scrolling down the opening page, you'll see several sections that include **Apps that we've picked for you**, **Top free apps**, **Top paid apps**, **Best-rated apps**, **New and rising apps**, **Collections** and **Categories**. If any of these are of interest, click the **Show all** link at the right of the section to see more. If you have an idea of what you are looking for, try clicking the **App categories** link at the top.

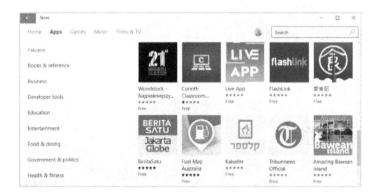

From the navigation bar at the left, click the category you are interested in. A list of related apps will open at the right side of the window.

Click on one to see what it's about.

At the top, you'll see a brief summary of what the apps does – click the **More** button for more details. Below that is the price of the app, followed by some screenshots of the app in action, Ratings and reviews, Features, Additional information, and Whats new in this version.

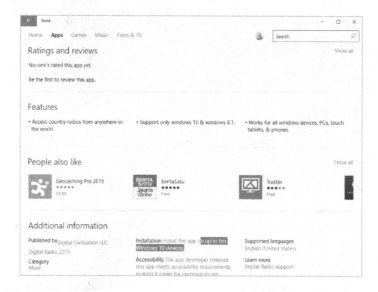

If you click on the screenshots, they'll open full-screen giving you a better view. Reading the ratings and reviews will give you a good idea of whether or not the app is good for its stated purpose.

Buying and Installing Apps

If you decide you want a particular app, proceed as follows:

1. Open the app's details screen and click the **Price** button

2. A window will open asking you to sign in by entering your Microsoft account password

3. A **Buy app** window will now open. Enter the requested details and then click the **Buy** button. The fee will be deducted from the credit card registered to your account. Some apps, of course, are free, in which case you won't have to go through the payment process

4. The app is now downloaded to your computer – you will see a progress bar on the screen. When the download is complete, it will be installed automatically – you don't have to do a thing

5. Still on the app's details screen, you will now see an **Open** button. Click it to open the app

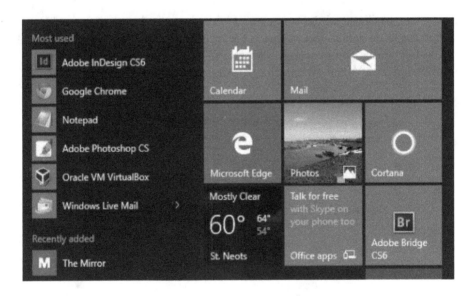

6. Alternatively, close the Store and open the Start menu. At the top, under the **Most used** section, you will now see a **Recently added** section. Your new app will be listed here – click to open it

After a while, the app will disappear from the **Recently added** section. From that point, you will have to access it by scrolling down to where it is listed under the appropriate letter in the Start menu. Initially, it will have a **New** tag appended to it.

Not everything you install on the computer will come from the Windows Store of course – you may have bought a traditional program from your local computer store. This will be in the form of a CD or DVD disc. The installation procedure in this case will be:

1. Place the disc in your computer's CD/DVD drive

2. Windows 10 will automatically look for an installation program on the disc. If it finds one, a pop-up window should open asking you to **Click to choose what happens with this disc.** If it does, click the window

3. If you don't see the pop-up window, open **This PC** and click on the **CD/DVD drive** to access the disc

4. The installation program should now open. If it doesn't, look for it on the disc – it will be labeled **Setup** or **Install** – click it

5. Follow the prompts to install the program – the procedure may vary slightly from program to program

In the case of a program downloaded from the Internet, do the following:

1. When the download is complete, at the bottom of the browser you will see this window

2. If you click **View downloads,** a nav bar will open at the right from where you will see a link to the Downloads folder where the program's setup file has been saved. Just click on it to initiate the installation procedure

3. Alternatively, click the **Run** button and follow the prompts

Keeping Track of Your Apps

Buying apps can become an addictive pastime and you may at some point wish to review what you have already bought. Trying to do it out from the Start menu will be tedious and time-consuming, so you will be pleased to know there is a better way.

1. Open the Windows Store and at the top, click this button

2. In the menu that opens, click **Purchased**

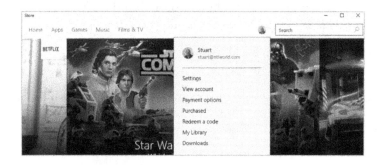

3. You will now be asked to sign in to your Microsoft account

4. Your Microsoft account will open in a browser window at the **Purchase history** page where you can see exactly what you have bought and when

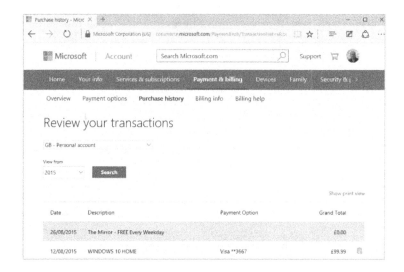

Uninstalling Apps

Previous editions of Windows have provided an uninstall facility called **Programs and Features**, which we look at below. Windows 10, however, makes it even easier by enabling apps to be uninstalled directly from the Start menu.

1. Open the Start menu and right-click on the app to be uninstalled

2. The right-click menu will show an **Uninstall** option – click it

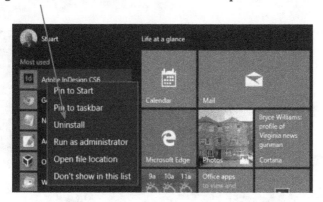

3. If it's a Windows 10 app, you'll now see a warning message stating **This app and its related info will be uninstalled** – click the **Uninstall** button to remove the app from the computer

However, if the app being uninstalled is not one of the new Windows 10 apps, the procedure will be slightly different. At Step 2, clicking the **Uninstall** button will open the Programs and Features utility in the Control Panel, which we mentioned above:

Locate the app in the Programs and Features window, right-click on it and click the **Uninstall** button. You will see a warning message asking if you are sure you want to uninstall it – click **Yes** and the app will be uninstalled.

Live Tiles

The default apps supplied with Windows 10 look somewhat different to the traditional Windows programs. Instead of each having a unique icon, they are all represented by a colored tile.

Many of these tiles are "live" meaning that instead of just showing an unchanging color, they display real-time information. A typical example is the News app as we see below:

By default, if an app tile has live functionality, it is activated. Should you not want this, you can turn it off by right-clicking on the tile and clicking **Turn live tile off** as we see below:

Apps that have live functionality are Mail, People, Calendar, Photos, Groove Music, News, Sport, and Money.

Note that with some of these apps, it will be necessary to set up a Microsoft account before the live functionality is available.

CHAPTER 7

Networking

The networking functionality built in to Windows 10 enables you to share all kinds of stuff with users of other computers.

Before you can do this though, it will be necessary to create a network. This chapter takes you through all the steps required to do it. You will learn what hardware is needed, how to set it up, and how to designate the files and folders to be shared.

Hardware Requirements

Most computers that exist in a family environment are used to share stuff such as pictures, music, emails, etc, between members of the family. However, sharing data doesn't have to be so restricted; it can actually be shared with any computer, anywhere in the world.

How is this possible? The answer is by setting up a network. This will, however, require a certain amount of hardware to be installed and set up on the computer. Networks come in two types: **Wired**, which uses network cables and **Wireless**, which uses wireless radio signals. For the home user, the latter is the best option and is the one we describe here. To get going, you will need:

- **A wireless network adapter** – this is a component that enables a PC to send and receive signals wirelessly. Many computers have this functionality built-in but not all do. To find out if yours does, open the Settings app from the Start menu and go to **Network & Internet**. If you see a **WiFi** option at the top of the window, you're good to go

If you don't see a **WiFi** option, you need to go out and buy a wireless adapter from your local computer store. These cost a few dollars and simply plug in to a USB port on the PC

- **A wireless router** – also known as a network controller, a router is a device that connects your computer to the Internet – wireless versions do it without the need for cabling. Many homes these days have a wireless router already installed as part of their broadband setup. If you don't have one though, as with the adapter, you'll need to acquire one and install it. The router will come with an installation disc that lets you set up the device and configure various security settings

Installing the Hardware

Installing and setting up computer hardware these days is far easier to do than it was a few years ago. Windows 10 automates much of the required routines leaving just a few configuration settings to be made by the user. However, for the uninitiated, we'll briefly run through the procedure.

We'll start with installing the network adapter:

1. Insert the installation disk into the CD/DVD drive

2. The device's setup program should now start automatically. If not, activate it as previously described

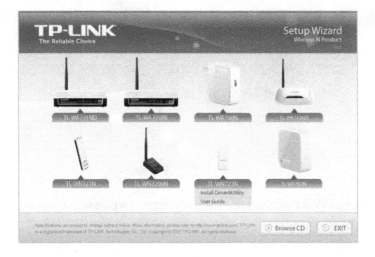

3. The installation disc will often contain setup programs for several different models; if this is the case with yours, select your model from the list

4. From this point on, it's largely a case of clicking **Next** buttons and granting permissions when requested

5. When the installation is complete, you will be instructed to connect the adapter to your computer

When it comes to installing a wireless router, the first step is to connect the device to a port at the rear of the computer with the supplied cable. Once done, insert the installation disc in the CD/DVD drive and simply follow the on-screen instructions.

You will be asked to specify a name and password for your wireless connection. This is important because unauthorized parties can easily connect to an unprotected network, and steal its bandwidth as well as the user's personal data.

Connecting to the Network

Hardware installed and configured, you now need to see if your computer has seen, or "discovered" your new network and, if so, connect to it.

Do this as follows:

1. Open the Settings app and click **Network & Internet**

2. If all has gone to plan, you will see a **WiFi** entry as shown below. This indicates the wireless network is up-and-running

3. Click the **WiFi** entry to open the connection window:

4. Click the **Connect** button to connect your computer to the network. When it is, the network will show as **Connected**

Note that in Step 4, you may be asked to enter a network security key. This can usually be found in the router's documentation or on a label on the device's casing

Network & Sharing Center

Windows provides a utility in the Control Panel that lets you see current network settings and change them if necessary.

1. Press the **Windows key + X** to open a menu at the bottom-left of the screen

2. Click **Control Panel** and then click **Network and Sharing Center**

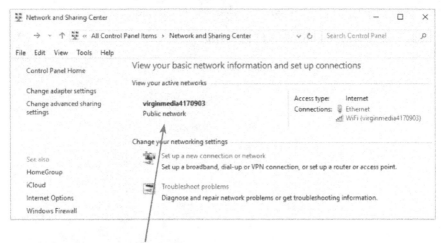

3. Details of the networks your computer is connected to are shown under **View your active networks**

4. Click the **WiFi** link at the right of **Connections:** to open a window that shows the connection's status

5. Click the **Properties** button to see the connection's WiFi details

Create a HomeGroup

A HomeGroup is essentially a link between two or more computers that are connected to the same network. Computers within the Homegroup can share content, and hardware such as a printer.

Creating a HomeGroup

Unlike some previous editions of Windows, Windows 10 does not provide a Homegroup by default. Therefore, you have to create one yourself:

1. Open the Control Panel via the **Winkey + X** menu

2. In the Control Panel, click **HomeGroup**

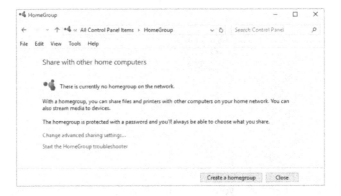

3. Click **Create a homegroup.** In the next window, click **Next**

4. In the next window, select the folders and devices you want to share with the Homegroup. Then click **Next**

5. In the final window, you will be given the password for the Homegroup. Make a note of it and then click the **Finish** button

Specify Files to Share

During the process of creating a homegroup, you are asked to specify the files you want to share with the group. The choice you are given is restricted to your computer's libraries – you can't be any more specific than that.

Once the Homegroup is set up, however, you have more options:

1. Open File Explorer

2. Browse to the folder containing the file, or files, you want to share with the Homegroup. In the example below, we have opened the Photos folder:

3   Select the files you want to share and then click the **Share** tab on the ribbon toolbar

4. Click the Homegroup the files are to be shared with – they will now be available for viewing by other members of the Homegroup

You can also stop the sharing of specific files in the same way. This time though, after selecting the files, click the **Stop sharing** button.

Troubleshooting Networks

There are any number of things that can bring a network down. To this end, Windows provides a useful troubleshooter that can resolve many of the issues that affect networks. So, if you experience problems with your homeGroup, your first move is to:

1. Open the Network and Sharing Center

2. Click **Troubleshoot problems**

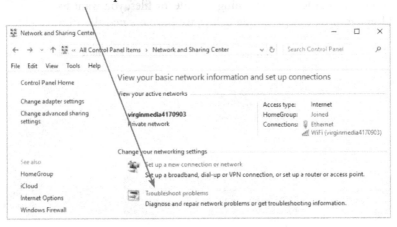

3. Select the type of problem you are experiencing

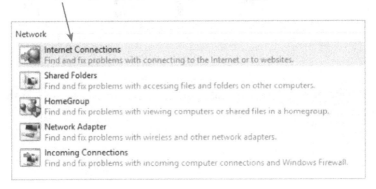

4. Windows will search its online troubleshooting database for likely solutions and inform you of any that it finds

CHAPTER 8

Customizing Windows 10

In Chapter 10, we see how to customize your computing environment to reflect your personality, mode of working, and preferences.

We explain how to change the visual look of Windows by changing the Desktop and Lock Screen backgrounds, the size of screen elements, the sounds it emits, accessibility options, and much more.

Desktop & Lock Screen Background

One of the first things that most people do when using a new operating system is to change the Desktop's background, or wallpaper, as it is more commonly known. It is also possible to change the Lock screen's background as well.

Desktop Background

To change the desktop wallpaper, do the following:

1. Right-click on an empty part of the Desktop and click **Personalize**

2. The Personalization window opens – click **Background**

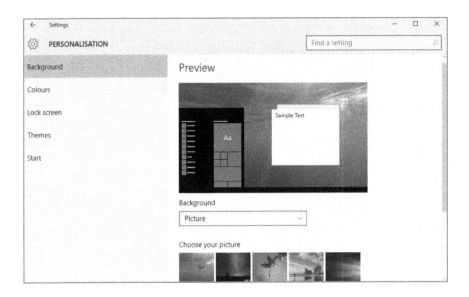

In the drop-down box under **Background,** you'll see three options: Picture, Solid Color, and Slideshow. Select the former and you'll be offered a choice of five default pictures. Below, you'll see a **Browse** button. Click this to open the Pictures folder in File Explorer. You can either select one from here or browse to another location and select one from there.

Select the Solid Color option to open a list of 24 colors. Just click one to set it as the desktop color.

The Slideshow option lets you play a slideshow on the Desktop. Click the **Browse** button to select albums from which the pictures for the slideshow will be taken. You can choose different time periods for the pictures to change.

At the bottom of the window, you'll be able to choose a fit if you have selected a picture as the background. Options include Fill, Fit, Stretch, Tile, Center and Span.

Lock Screen Background

To change how the Lock Screen looks:

1. In the Personalization window, click **Lock screen** at the left

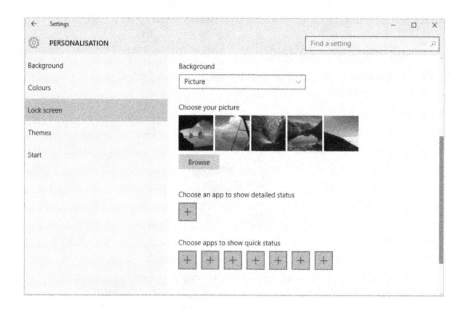

With the Lock screen, you have just two options: Picture or Slideshow. As with the Desktop, click the **Browse** button to select the required picture, or pictures, for either option.

Something that is available for the Lock screen but not for the Desktop is notifications – these provide real-time updates on various events. The Lock screen Personalization window lets you specify which apps you want to show these notifications.

You will be able to choose one app to show detailed information, and up to seven to show basic information. Just click in the + boxes to open the list of apps on your computer.

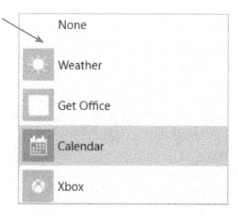

Right at the bottom of the window, you'll see a **Screen timeout settings** link. This lets you specify the time after which the PC's screen is turned off, and after which it is put to sleep.

Screensavers

A screensaver is a simple program that fills the screen with moving images or patterns when the computer is not in use. Initially designed to prevent phosphor burn-in on CRT and plasma monitors, screensavers are now used primarily for entertainment, security or to display system status information.

To set up a screensaver on your Windows 10 computer:

1. Type **screensaver** into the Taskbar search box and press **Enter**

2. The Screen Saver Settings screen opens as shown below:

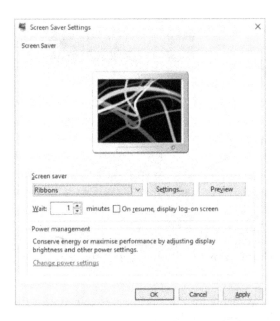

3. Click the drop-down box to select the required screensaver. As you select one, you will see a mini-preview in the small screen above. To see a full-screen preview, click the **Preview** button. Move the mouse to end the preview

4. Some of the screensavers have settings that can be adjusted. To see what these are, select the screensaver and then click the **Settings** button

5. Below the drop-down box, you'll see a **Wait:** box. If you want to specify a time before the screensaver activates, enter it here. You can either type in the required time or set it with the up/down arrows.

Windows 10 does not supply a great choice of screensavers. However, you can download many more from the Internet. Many of them are far more complex and useful as well.

Themes

On a related note, we have Themes. A theme is a combination of pictures, colors, and sounds. It includes a desktop background, a screensaver, a window border color, and a sound scheme. Some themes also include desktop icons and mouse pointers.

Themes provide a quick way of customizing the look and sound of your computer. Several themes are provided with Windows 10 but if you don't like any of these, you can find literally hundreds online.

To see what Windows 10 has to offer:

1. Right-click on an empty part of the desktop and click **Personalize**

2. The Personalization window opens – click **Themes**

3. Click **Theme settings** on the right of the window

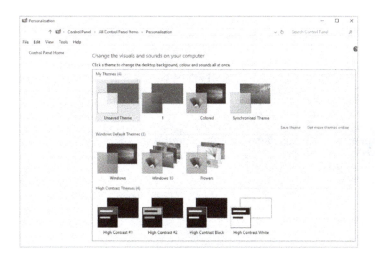

Windows 10 provides three default themes for normal usage – just click one to activate it. Below, you'll see four High Contrast themes that are intended for people who don't see too well.

It is also possible to alter the default themes, and to create your own. To do the latter, just activate one of the default themes and then make the changes you want to it, i.e. the Desktop and Lock screen backgrounds, the computer's sound effects, the mouse pointer, icon size – there are any number of things you can customize.

When you have things just as you want them, go back to the Personalization screen and click **Save Theme**. Give your new theme a name and then click the **Save** button. It can now be selected or deselected at any time.

Sounds

Most computers these days come with a separate volume control. If not, you can always use the one supplied by Windows 10. Type **volume** into the Taskbar search box and press **Enter** to open the system volume control:

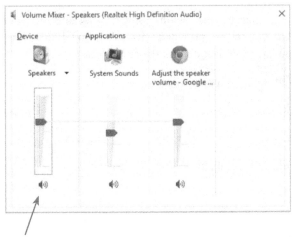

This lets you adjust the volume of the computer's speakers, plus the volume of system sounds – those jingles and clicks you hear from time to time. (The author has Google's Chrome browser installed, hence the Google Chrome volume control at the right.)

Now open the Control Panel and click **Sound**:

Click the **Sounds** tab. The drop-down box under **Sound Scheme** lets you select from a large number of sound schemes.

Under **Program Events,** you will see a list of all the Windows clicks and jingles and the events that generate them.

Click any of these events and then apply a different sound to it from the drop-down box under **Sounds** at the bottom.

You can preview all the sounds by clicking the **Test** button. Finally, click the **Apply** button.

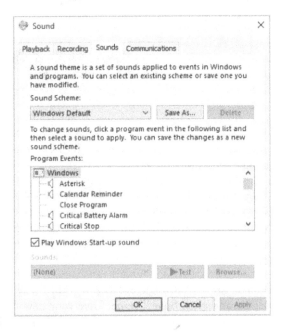

Icons & Tiles

Like just about everything else in Windows, even the Desktop icons and Start menu tiles can be customized.

Desktop Icons
To change the size of the Desktop icons, right-click on the Desktop and, from the menu, select **View**.

You'll see three size options: Small, Medium, and Large. Make your choice and it will be applied immediately.

Should you want to, you can remove all the icons from the Desktop by unchecking **Show desktop icons**.

You can also change some system Desktop icons. Type **desktop icons** into the Taskbar search box and press **Enter**. You will see this screen:

Click one of the icons in the main window and then click **Change Icon**. A window will open with a scrollable list of dozens of alternative icons that you can use. Just select one and click **OK**.

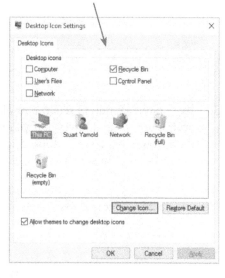

At the top of the window, checking and unchecking the boxes will add or remove the associated icons from the Desktop.

Tiles
It is also possible to change the size of the Start menu tiles. To do this, right-click on the tile to open the menu shown below:

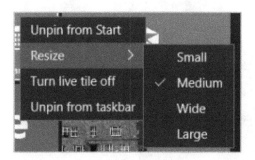

Select from the options offered: Small, Medium, Wide and Large.

The Wide option will double the width of the tile, while the Large option will double it in both width and height.

Screen Resolution

The resolution of your monitor screen affects the size of the items it displays. If it is set too high, it could well be that icons and text will be too small to be read comfortably, and vice versa. Set it to your liking as follows:

1. Type **resolution** in to the Taskbar search box and press **Enter**

2. The **Advanced Display Settings** window will open

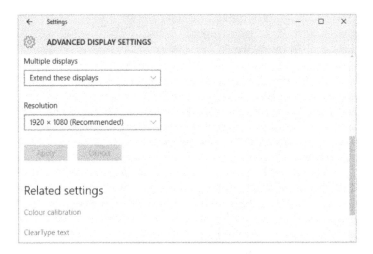

3. By default, Windows sets the resolution to what it considers to be the optimum setting. However, if you wish to try a different setting, open the drop-down menu under **Resolution**.

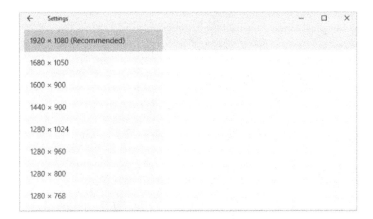

4. The resolutions your monitor is capable of displaying are shown in the list. Select one and then click **Apply**

ClearType

ClearType font technology delivers improved font display quality over traditional forms of font smoothing or anti-aliasing. ClearType improves readability on color LCD displays with a digital interface, such as those in laptops and tablets.

It's on by default in Windows 10, but you can fine-tune the settings as we explain below:

1. Type **cleartype** into the Taskbar search box and press **Enter**

2. At the opening screen, click **Next**

3. At the second screen, Windows checks that you are using the correct (native) resolution for your monitor. Click **Next**

4. There then follows a series of screens showing different views of a sample of text

5. Select the sample that looks best to you and click **Next**. At the final screen, click **Finish** to exit the ClearType tuner – your selection will now be applied

While not for everybody, many people will find that ClearType can improve the legibility of screen text considerably.

Accessibility Options

Many people have disabilities that make it difficult to use a computer. For these users, Windows 10 provides a range of accessibility options that can make a big difference to their use of the computer.

Discover what options are available by typing **ease** in to the Taskbar search box and pressing **Enter**. The **Ease of Access Center** opens:

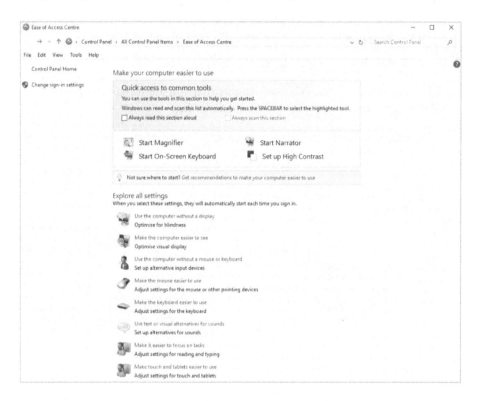

You will see many options here so if you're a bit confused we suggest you click the yellow **Not sure where to start?** box. This opens a question and answer screen that gives Windows some information regarding your disabilities. It will then make recommendations based on the information you have provided.

Alternatively, right at the top of the screen, you'll see some commonly used accessibility tools. These include:

- **Magnifier** – when activated, Magnifier will run when you log on to your computer. Magnifier enlarges the part of the screen where the mouse is pointing and can be particularly useful for viewing objects that are difficult to see

- **Narrator** – Narrator reads aloud on-screen text and describes events (such as error messages appearing) that happen while you're using the computer

- **On-Screen Keyboard** – the on-screen keyboard displays a visual keyboard with all the standard keys. You can select keys using the mouse or another pointing device, or you can use a single key, or group of keys, to cycle through the keys on the screen

- **High Contrast** – this option lets you set a high-contrast color scheme that heightens the color contrast of some text and images on your computer screen, thus making those items more distinct and easier to identify

Moving down the screen, you'll see some more accessibility options. These include:

- **Use the computer without a display** – clicking this opens a screen that offers a range of accessibility aids designed to help the blind. These include Narrator and Audio description

- **Make the computer easier to see** – this is for those whose eyesight is poor. Options include High contrast color scheme, Narrator, Audio description, Magnifier, thickness of the blinking cursor, and more

- **Use the computer without a mouse or keyboard** – for people who cannot use a physical keyboard, this screen offers options for activating an on-screen keyboard and using speech recognition

- **Make the mouse easier to use** – this screen provides options for changing the color and size of the mouse pointer, using mouse keys (controlling the mouse with the numeric keypad), and activating windows by mouse hover

- **Make the keyboard easier to use** – options on this screen include turning on Sticky keys, Mouse keys, Toggle keys, and Filter keys

- **Use text or visual alternatives for sounds** – for people who are deaf, options here provide visual cues to replace sounds. These include flashing active captions bars, flashing active window and flashing Desktop

- **Make it easier to focus on tasks** – options here help to reduce the amount of information on your screen so that it's easier to read. Aids include Narrator, Sticky keys, Toggle keys, and turning off unnecessary animations

- **Make touch and tablets easier to use** – this option lets you specify an accessibility tool to be launched when the Windows and volume buttons are pressed simultaneously

Date & Time

For those of you who like to be on time, Windows 10 offers a Date and Time utility that can be accessed in the Control Panel.

The utility opens on the Date and Time tab, which gives you options to change the date and the time, and to change the time zone.

The Additional Clocks tab lets you create additional clocks to display the time in other time zones. These can be viewed by clicking on or hovering the mouse over the Taskbar clock.

The Internet Time tab lets you synchronize your computer with a number of Internet time servers to make sure it is dead on time.

Select a time server from the Server: drop-down box and then click the **Update now** button.

Your computer's time will now be reset to that of the server. You can set this to happen automatically by checking the **Synchronize with an Internet time server**

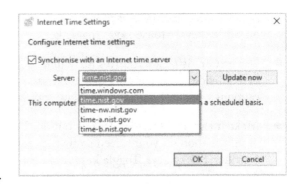

checkbox. By default, this is done once a week. This does of course rely on a reliable Internet connection – no connection, no update. You may also want to check that your firewall is not blocking the synchronization.

CHAPTER 9

The Internet

Windows 10 introduces a new web browser. This is called Edge and it replaces Internet Explorer.

Edge is designed to be lightweight with a layout engine built around current web standards. It removes support for legacy technologies such as ActiveX in favor of extensions and integration with other Microsoft services, such as the digital assistant Cortana and OneDrive.

The Edge Web Browser

For two decades, the default web browser in Windows has been Internet Explorer. Over the years, this browser has become bloated, insecure, and confusing to use.

For these reasons, a lot of people are using alternatives such as Google Chrome. With Windows 10, Microsoft has gone back to the drawing board and scrapped everything it had done so far with Internet Explorer. It has come up with an entirely new browser from scratch, one that is intended to shed all of the baggage of Internet Explorer and so offer a modern, fast web browsing experience for Windows users. Edge has been built to be clean, tight, and responsive.

Internet Explorer is still alive – just – and is also supplied with Windows 10. However, it's buried away in the operating system and Microsoft says that's largely for compatibility with legacy enterprise apps.

Edge is the default browser, and it is available across Microsoft's product line, from computers to smartphones to Holo Lens and Surface Hub.

One of the new browser's coolest features is integration with Cortana, which pops up here and there as you browse with Edge, providing context when you highlight a word and choose **Ask Cortana**; or when you type in queries for weather and other common search terms in Edge's search bar.

Edge has other new features. A reading list lets you save articles and web pages for later reading, though it doesn't work offline. Edge can present a page in a stripped-down format that removes ads and extraneous banners for easier reading, similar to Apple's Safari browser on OS X. A note-taking mode lets you doodle on and mark up a web page, then save that image to OneNote or share it with another app.

However, it doesn't have a number of the power features that Chrome and Firefox users have long been accustomed to. It doesn't yet support extensions or plug-ins (the former are coming later this year and in a format that's very similar to Google's Chrome App Store).

Currently, there's no way to sync your browsing history or favorite sites with your mobile device. Edge also doesn't work too well with Google's web apps, so if you're a diehard Google Docs or Sheets user, you'll want to stick to Chrome. Microsoft's own Office web apps work well, however.

As it stands, Edge is not quite as good or feature-complete as it could be (which can also be said for Windows 10 as a whole at this point). That said, it's an excellent start and already much better than Internet Explorer.

Main Elements

The first thing you notice when you open Edge is it's simple, uncluttered and clean design. Lets take a look at the browser's main elements:

Forward, Back and Refresh | New tab | Tab bar | Reading View | Add to favorites or reading list

Address bar | Page window | Hub | Web note | Share | More

Edge's performance in comparison to other popular browsers is shown below:

Benchmark	IE 11 (Jan)	Spartan (Jan)	Edge 20 (July)	Chrome 40 (Jan)	Chrome 43 (July)	Firefox 35 (Jan)	Firefox 39 (July)
Browser Performance							
Sunspider (lower is better)	149.7ms	144.6ms	**133.4ms**	260.9ms	247.5ms	220.1ms	234.6ms
Octane 2.0 (higher is better)	9861	17928	**22278**	17474	19407	16508	19012
Kraken 1.1 (lower is better)	3781.2ms	2077.5ms	**1797.9ms**	1992.8ms	1618.7ms	1760.4ms	1645.5ms
WebXPRT (higher is better)	913	1083	**1132**	1251	1443	1345	1529
Oort Online (higher is better)	1990	2170	**5470**	5370	7620	3900	7670*
HTML5Test (higher is better)	339	344	**402**	511	526	449	467

Create Your Home Page

When you open Edge, by default, it opens at a page of its own choosing. Few users are going to put up with this, so below we explain how to configure Edge to open at a page determined by you.

1. Click the **More actions** ⋯ button at the top-right of the browser

2. Click **Settings**

3. The **Start page** option is selected by default.

4. Deselect the **Start page** option by clicking the **A specific page or pages** radio button

5. A drop-down box opens here. Click in it and select the **Custom** option

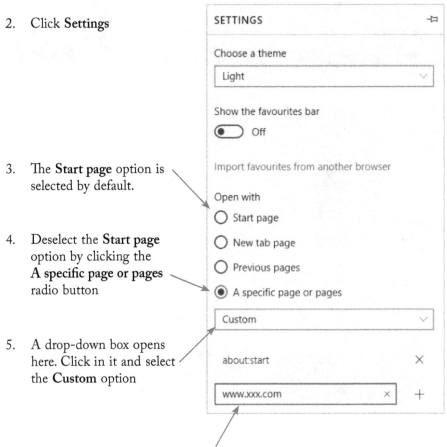

SETTINGS

Choose a theme

Light

Show the favourites bar

Off

Import favourites from another browser

Open with

○ Start page

○ New tab page

○ Previous pages

◉ A specific page or pages

Custom

about:start   ✕

www.xxx.com   ✕   +

6. Enter the website that you want Edge to open when you start it up. Finish by clicking on the + button

From now on, every time you start Edge it will open at the specified web page.

Opening a Web Page

To open a web page with Edge, you first have to enter an address. This is done with the browsers "smart address bar" (these are now common in modern browsers).

They are called "smart" because they offer more than just one function. The address bar in Edge lets you enter the required address, open the page at the address, and can also be used as a search box.

By default, it is hidden away – in the screenshot below there is no sign of an address bar.

Click on where you'd expect the address bar to be though and it will magically appear as we see below:

To use the address bar, just start typing the address of the site you want to visit – as you do so, a list appears below showing suggested web sites and search suggestions – this is the bar carrying out two functions at the same time.

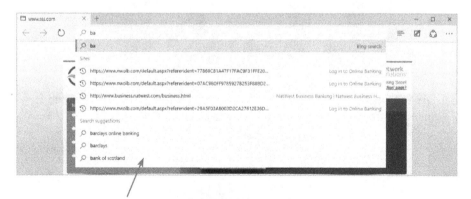

If one of the suggestions is what you are looking for, click on it to go the page. You can also use the personal assistant, Cortana, to open web pages. Just speak the web site's address into your microphone and Edge will open the site.

Working With Tabs

Tabbed browsing is a feature found on all modern web browsers. It lets you have a number of web pages open at the same time and quickly switch between them by clicking the appropriate tab.

1. Open Edge

2. Right at the top of the browser window is the Tab bar

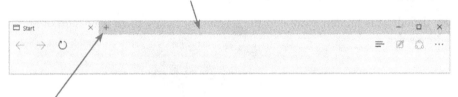

3. Click the + button to open a tab

4. In the new tab, enter the address of the required web page in the address bar or click one of the **Top sites** listed in the main window

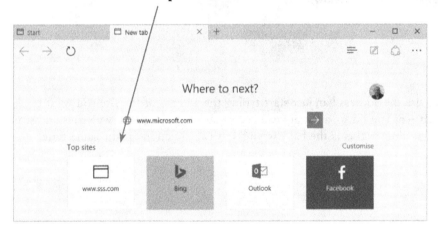

5. As you open more tabs, they are added to the Tab bar. Each open tab is named after the site open in it – this lets you distinguish between them

6. To open a tab, just click on it

Some useful tab features include being able to rearrange tabs on the bar by dragging them left and right. Right-clicking on an element in a page reveals an option to open that element in a new tab. Also, you can change the default Start page when a tab is opened – you'll find this option in Edge's settings.

Favorites

Everyone who uses the Internet regularly will have sites they visit much more often than others. You can save yourself the bother of having to type the address of these sites each time you want to visit them by making use of your browser's Favorites feature.

Creating Favorites

1. With the site open, click the **Add to favorites or reading list** button

2. The page's name is entered in the **Name** box – change this if you want to

3. By default, the favorite is created in the Favorites folder. By clicking **Create new folder** below, you can create your own Favorites folder. The ability to do this can be useful when you have a lot of favorites and they need to be organized

5. When you're ready to save the favorite, click the **Add** button

Opening Favorites

Having created a favorite, you now need some way of accessing it. Look at Edge's interface and you'll see no obvious way to do it. The solution is twofold:

● You can access your favorites via Edge's Hub feature, which we look at on page 119

● You can open a Favorites toolbar that sits just under the address bar and provides instant access. Do this as follows:

    1. Click the **More actions** button at the top-right of the browser and then click **Settings**. Click **Show the favorites bar** to **On**

    2. The empty Favorites bar appears under the address bar

    3. You now have to move your current favorites to the Favorites bar. Open each favorite, click the **Favorite** button, select **Favorites Bar** and then click **Update**. You can, of course, save your favorites directly to the Favorites bar as you create them

Reading Lists

The Reading List feature in Edge provides you with a place to save articles or other content that you want to read later – on the bus, over the weekend – wherever and whenever you like. As the content is saved on the computer or tablet, an Internet connection is not required to read it.

To save an article in your reading list:

1.   Open the web page that you want to add to your reading list

2.   Click the **Add to favorites or reading list** button on the toolbar

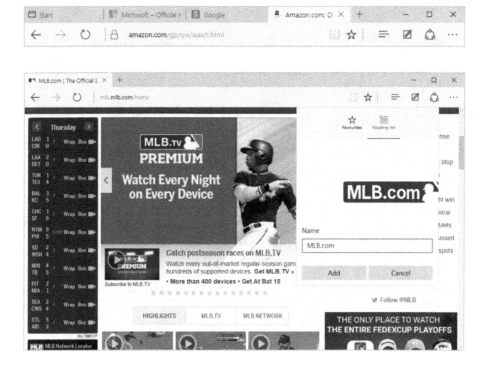

3.   Click the **Reading List** tab. If you want to, you can rename the link in the **Name** box provided. Then click the **Add** button

4.   Saved articles can be opened later on via Edge's Hub feature as we explain on page 119

As it stands, the Reading List feature is rather basic as you can only save links to it. You do not have the option to create folders, or to auto-delete items after a specified number of days.

Reading View

On many web pages these days, it is difficult to find the content – the reason you opened the page in the first place – due to the proliferation of extraneous web objects such as video clips, ads, and banners. Sometimes, the content can be enhanced by it but, more often than not, it is just a pain in the ass.

The Reading View feature provided by Edge solves this problem by stripping out all content other than the article itself.

To use it:

1. Open the web page containing the article that you want to read. It will probably be loaded with ads and stuff just like this one

2. Click the **Reading View** button

3. Read the article in peace and quite with nothing to distract you

Notes

Edge lets you take notes, write, doodle, and highlight directly on web pages as a note. Afterwards, you can save or share the web note. Lets see how to use the Notes feature:

1. Open the web page and click the **Make a Web Note** button

2. The toolbar and tab will turn maroon in color, indicating that you are currently viewing, or making, a web note on the page. At the top-left of the browser, you will see five buttons. From left to right, these are: Pen, Highlighter, Eraser, Note, and Clip

3. Click the **Pen** button once to open the pen. Double-click to open a small menu from where you can select the pen size and the ink color

4. Click the **Note** button and then click on the page. A small note window will open as we see below:

5. Write your note

6. Another option is provided by the **Clip** tool. Click the **Clip** button and then you will be able to draw a rectangle around any part of the screen you want to save as a note

7. Having written your note or clip, you now need to click the **Save Web Note** button at the right of the maroon toolbar. Save options include sending it to OneNote or saving in Edge's Favorites or Reading List

The Hub

The Hub is a central location within Edge that is used to store a number of different things. It enables you to find them quickly and works as follows:

1. On Edge's toolbar, click the Hub button

2. A sidebar will open with four buttons at the top. From left to right, these are: Favorites, Reading List, History, and Downloads

Favorites

We described how the Favorites feature in Edge works on page 115. Saved favorites can be viewed via the Favorites bar that can be placed on the browser window and also in the Hub. Just open the Hub and click the **Favorites** button.

Reading list

We described how to add content to the Reading List on page 116. In order to access and read that content, you need to open the Hub and click the **Reading list** button. It shows a chronological list of all the content you have saved for later reading. Having read an article, you can delete it from your device by right-clicking and clicking **Remove.**

History

Click the **History** button and you will be presented with a detailed history of your web browsing activities. Details of every site you have visited, plus the date and time are all recorded and available for viewing from the list. You can delete the entire list by clicking the **Clear all history** link at the top-right, and individual entries via the right-click menu.

Downloads

The Downloads button opens a list of everything you have downloaded to your computer. That's it really – you have no options here other than to see what has been downloaded.

As a final note, you can pin any of the above in a permanently open view by clicking the **Pin** icon.

Private Browsing

Online security is a very important issue these days, and in more ways than one. Yes, we all want to keep hackers out of our bank accounts and big corporations from snooping through our emails. But there's also the issue of browsing the Internet – how can we keep this private?

The answer to this comes in the form of Edge's InPrivate browsing feature. To get going with this:

1.   Open the browser

2.   Click the **More actions** button

3.   Click **New InPrivate window**

4.   A new browser window will open. It will look and act exactly the same as a regular browser window does. The only indication you will have that you are in InPrivate mode is the **InPrivate** label at the top-left of the browser window

When you exit InPrivate mode, all the data that Edge has collected during the session is deleted from the computer. Information that is discarded includes cookies, temporary Internet files, web page history, form data and passwords, and the anti-phishing cache to mention just some.

As a result, you are able to surf the web without leaving an electronic trail that anyone with the requisite knowledge and/or tools can follow.

Pinning Sites

A cool feature available in Edge is "Pinning". This lets you pin a web page to the computer's Start menu. Once done, you can then go to the page immediately without having to start up Edge first.

Do it as follows:

1. Open Edge and go to the page you want to pin

2. Click the **More actions** button and click **Pin to Start**

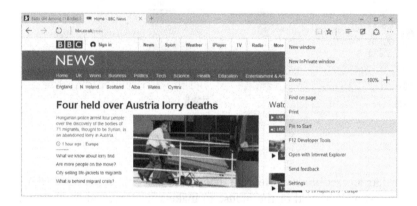

3. Close Edge and go to the Start menu on the computer. Look in the tile section at the right and you will find a tile that shows the web site's logo

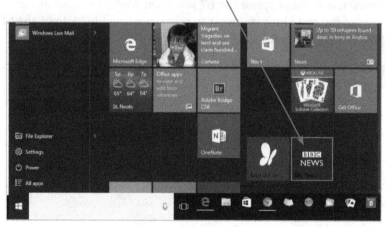

4. Click the tile and Edge will open the page in a new browser window. Note that this will be a live tile and so it may display real-time information that is regularly updated

Caret Browsing

When selecting text in a web page, it can be difficult to select precisely what you want without also selecting adjacent text, and objects such as images and tables, as we see in the example below:

Edge offers a caret browsing feature that solves this problem. It enables you to use the keyboard instead of the mouse to make selections, and it offers more precise control.

You can activate caret browsing in the browser's Advanced settings. A quicker way, however, is to simply press the **F7** key. Then place the cursor at the beginning of the text block you want to select, press and hold down the **Shift** key and highlight the text with the arrow keys.

Some users may find this feature so useful that they might want to have caret browsing permanently enabled.

To do this:

1. Click the **More actions** button and click **Settings**

2. Scroll down and click **View advanced settings**

3. Click the **Always use caret browsing** switch to **On**

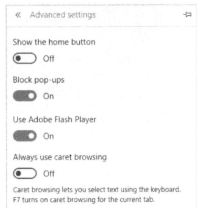

Change Search Provider

By default, all searches conducted with the Edge browser will be done with Microsoft's Bing search engine. If you are happy with this, fine. If not, you can specify your own choice of search provider.

To do it:

1. Click the **More actions** button and click **Settings**

2. Scroll down and click **View advanced settings**

3. Click in the **Search in the address bar with** drop-down box

4. Click **Add new**

5. In the **Add a search provider** window, select your preferred provider from the ones listed by clicking on it

6. Click **Add as default**. From this point on, all searches will be done with the selected search provider

7. There is also an **Add** option. Selecting this will add the selected provider to Edge's search provider list – Bing will still be the default provider but you be able to use the other provider on a temporary basis.

   When the session done with this provider is closed, subsequent searches revert to Bing

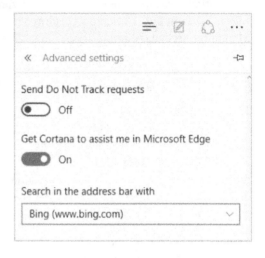

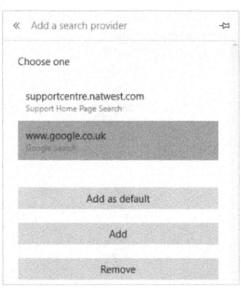

Browser Settings

We've highlighted some of the many settings available for the Edge browser in this chapter. To see what other settings are available, click the **More Actions** ⋯ button at the top far-right of the browser and then click **Settings**.

Reading
Two options are available here – **Reading view style** – you can choose between Light, Medium and Dark; and **Reading view font size** – choose between Small, Medium, Large and Extra Large.

Both of these will be useful for users whose eyesight is perhaps not quite as good as they'd like.

Block Pop-ups
Click Advaned Settings. Pop-ups are advertisement windows that appear as you browse through a web page. They are usually a complete pain in the ass and having them automatically blocked is perhaps not a bad thing. You may, however, prefer you to make your own mind up about this rather Microsoft doing it for you – if so, you can disable the automatic blocking by clicking the **Block pop-ups** switch to **Off**.

Privacy and services
There are two options here, both enabled by default, that you ought to consider. The **Offer to save passwords** and **Save form entries** options are potential security risks as another person who uses the computer will be able to access your password-protected pages, and to auto-fill various types of online forms.

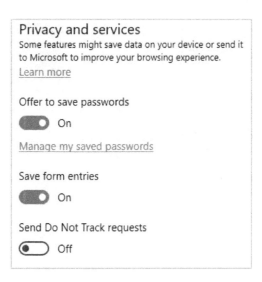

It depends what you use your computer for but our recommendation is that you disable both of these options by clicking their respective switches to **Off**.

CHAPTER 10

Email

In Chapter 10, we look at how you can use your computer to communicate with the world outside via email. We show you everything you need to know in this respect – types of email account, how to set up an email account, and how to use the email app supplied with Windows 10.

A related application is People, which provides you with a digital address book – we explain how to use this to the best effect.

Mail App

Windows 8 featured a very basic app for email, which was improved in 8.1 with things like drag-and-drop for moving mail among folders. The new Windows 10 Mail app that replaces it is actually part of the free version of Microsoft's Office Mobile productivity suite.

It's called Outlook Mail on Windows 10 Mobile running on smartphones and tablets, but just plain Mail on Windows 10 for computers. The email app comes with touch support and a new minimalist, flat design, and is a big advance over the Windows 8.1 Mail app.

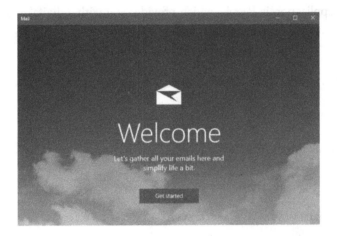

If you need to set up an mail account for the first time, the Mail client supports all the standard email systems, including Outlook.com, Exchange, Gmail, Yahoo! Mail, iCloud, and any POP or IMAP account you may have.

Simply enter your address and password for any of the account types, and Mail will figure out the required server settings. A big advantage of using Mail instead of the web browser version of your email is that new messages will appear in the Action Center's notifications pane, from which you can reply.

Mail's interface is minimalist and clean, and gets out of the way so you can concentrate on your email's contents. While it is designed for touch, using it with a keyboard and mouse is completely natural and fluid. It's a clear interface that works well in either setting.

The ability to connect multiple accounts, and fluid formatting and insertion choices, mean it's up to all but the most demanding email tasks. The integration with the Action Center is another plus for the app, as is the fact that once you set it up on one Windows 10 device, any others you sign into will require no setup whatsoever.

Email Accounts

Before you can use the Mail app, you must first set up an email account or add an existing one to it. This is very easy to do – if you currently use one of the popular email services such as iCloud, Gmail, Yahoo, etc, it's even easier as much of the work is already done for you – a few clicks are all that's needed.

If you decide to use a different service though, such as the one from your ISP, you will need to provide more information.

Email Services and Protocols

Most email services are web-based and use the IMAP protocol (except for Microsoft Exchange, which uses the MAPI protocol).

The Mail app in Windows 10 knows how to connect to all these services – all you need to supply is the email address and account password. If, however, you don't use any of these services, you will have to supply more information.

Apart from the email address and account password, you will also need to provide the names of the incoming and outgoing mail servers, plus any security info required to send email. You will also need to specify if the account is POP or IMAP.

All this information will be available from your email service provider – just ask them for it and you'll be ready to go. However, before we go into the mechanics of setting up an email account, we'll explain the difference between the email protocols, POP and IMAP.

- **POP (Post Office Protocol)** – with POP, emails are stored temporarily on your Internet Service Provider's (ISP's) server. When you connect to the server, the messages are downloaded to your computer and then deleted from the server

  The advantage of POP is that because all your emails are stored on the computer, they can be re-read at any time without the need to reconnect to the server. The disadvantage is that they can only be viewed on the computer to which they were downloaded

- **IMAP (Internet Message Access Protocol)** – IMAP essentially works the other way. Messages are not downloaded to your computer (although it may seem as though they are). They are actually stored permanently on the ISP's server and you simply read them from there

  The advantage with this method is that your email can be accessed via any device regardless of its location. The disadvantage is that in order to do so, an Internet connection is necessary

Setting Up an Email Account

Before you can use the Mail app, you need to set it up with an email account. This can be an existing account or a brand new one. We'll see how to set up an existing account as most people these days already have one.

1. Open the Start menu and click the **Mail** app

2. Click the **Get started** button

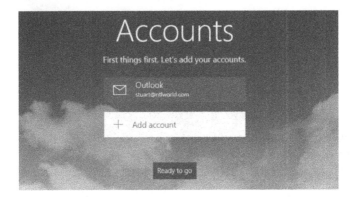

3. Click **Add account**

4. In the **Choose an account** window, select who your account is with – Google, Yahoo, etc. If none of them apply, click the **Other account** option

5. A sign-in window will open – just enter your email address and password in the boxes provided. Then click the **Sign-in** button

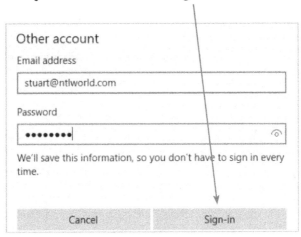

6. Assuming your details check out, your email account is set up with Mail without further ado – you're good to go

Receiving Email

With your email account set up, incoming messages will be received by the Mail app. The number of unread emails is indicated by the number at the right of the Inbox.

Email folders   Selected email   Message window

Unread emails   Inbox

When you click the Mail app on the Start menu, it will open as shown above. Your email folders are at the left, the Inbox is in the middle, and the message window is at the right.

To read a message just click on it in the Inbox and it will open in the message window at the right of the screen.

Unread emails are indicated by a blue horizontal bar at the left of the email in the Inbox.

To see all messages that haven't been read yet, click the **All** button at the top of the Inbox and then click **Unread** from the menu. Having caught up with your emails, click **Unread** and then click **All** to return to the normal Inbox view

To check for new email, click the **Sync this view** button on the toolbar. When the check is complete, you will see an **Up to date** message at the bottom of the Inbox.

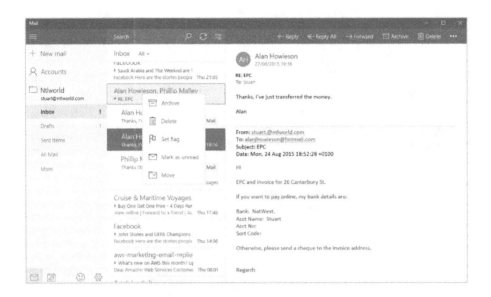

Right-click on any message in the Inbox to reveal these options:

- **Archive** – archiving a message removes it from the Inbox but doesn't delete it – you can access it whenever you need to

- **Delete** – removes the email from the Mail app

- **Set Flag** – flags the email in the Inbox by turning it yellow

- **Mark as unread** – places a blue horizontal bar at the front of the email to indicate it hasn't been read yet

- **Move** – this option opens a list of all the email folders in the account. Choose one to move the email to

All of these options are also available at the right of the toolbar. Click the **Actions** button at the far-right to reveal options for printing the email, and zooming in and out of the message window.

At the left of the toolbar, clicking the **Collapse** button will collapse the sidebar showing the email folders – the text labels will disappear leaving just the icons on show.

Directly above the Inbox is a search box. Click in it, enter your search term and then click the **magnifying glass** button to begin the search.

Finally, at the top of the Inbox, at the right, you will see a **Enter selection mode** button. Clicking it opens selection checkboxes next to each email.

Sending Email

Sending email messages with the Mail app is very straightforward. It may not provide some of the features and options found in more complex email clients such as Microsoft Outlook and Mozilla Thunderbird, but the ones it does provide are perfectly adequate as we will see.

Composing an Email Message

To write an email message, open the Mail app; it will open at the last received message. At the top-left of the screen tap the **+ New mail** button. A new message window will open at the right as shown below:

1. In the **To:** field, type the address. As you type, matching contacts from the People app appear in a window – if the one you want is there, click it and it will be entered automatically

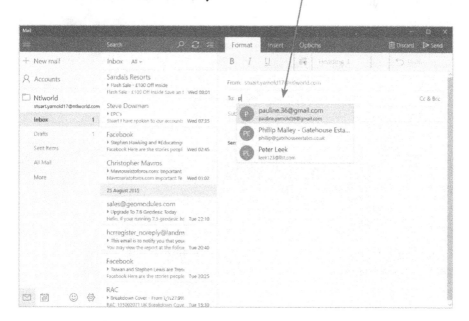

2. Click in the **Subject** field and then the type the subject (if there is one)

3. Click in the **Message** field (below the Subject field) and type your message. When you are ready to send it, click the **Send** button at the far-right of the toolbar

Formatting an Email Message

The Mail app in Windows 10 offers a good range of formatting options. These are all available from the Formatting toolbar that automatically opens when you open a message window as we see below:

Formatting options include Bold, Italics and Underline. Click the down-arrow to the left of these to open the menu of font related options shown on the right.

From the drop-down menu at the top, you can select from a range of fonts and font sizes. You can apply colored highlighting to selected sections of text with the Highlight tool, while the Font color tool lets you change the color of the text.

Next to the Font options button is the Paragraph formatting button.

Options provided here include bullets – type, shape and size; numbering – a range of numbering layouts; indents, text alignment and justification, line spacing, and paragraph spacing.

Finally, you can select from a list of different Headings by clicking the down-arrow to the right of **Heading 1**.

This includes headings of different fonts, font sizes, different colors, and italicized headings.

Sending Attachments

Sometimes you will want to attach something to an email – this can be a picture, a document or a link. The Mail app has this covered as well:

On the Formatting toolbar, click the **Insert** tab to reveal the following options:

Attach – clicking the **Attach** button opens the Documents folder in File Explorer – if the document you want to send is here, just click it and it will be attached to the email. If not, use File Explorer to browse to where it is located.

Table – clicking **Table** inserts a table into the body of the email. You will now see different, table-related, options on the toolbar.

Pictures – as with the Attach option, clicking **Pictures** opens the Documents folder. Browse to where the required picture is located, click it and it will be inserted into the body of the email.

Different options will now be available on the toolbar – these will let you rotate, crop, and resize the picture

Link – if you wish to send a link to a web page in an email, click the **Link** option. This will open a box into which you can enter the address of the link and also a name for it.

Options

The last tab on the formatting toolbar is Options. This lets you specify an importance level for the email – either High or Low. You can also set the language of the text used in the email from the Language drop-down box. If, like the author, your spelling ability is not too good, click **Spelling** to run a spell check on what you have written.

Create a Signature

By default, every email you send from the Mail app will be signed "Sent from Mail for Windows 10". Change this as follows:

1. At the bottom-right of the email folders sidebar, you will see a **Switch to settings** button. Click this and then click **Options**

2. Under Signature, either switch it off or enter your own in the signature box

Using Contacts

All computing devices these days provide an address book in which you can store contact details of the people in your life. The version offered by Window 10 is the People app.

The People and Mail apps are inextricably linked – start typing an address into an email and Mail will immediately query the People app to see if it is holding an address for it. If so, it will appear in a window from where you can select it.

However, for this to work, the address must be in the People app in the first place. Lets see how to do this.

Create a Contact Manually

The People app is very simple and creating an entry couldn't be easier:

1. On the Start menu, click **People**

2. The app opens – click the + button at the top-left of the window

3. A New contact window opens – enter the contact's details in the fields provided

4. If a required field isn't available, scroll down and click + **Other** to open a list of more fields from which you can choose

5. If you have a photo of the contact, click **Add photo** at the top-left of the window – this opens the Photos app. Find the picture, select it, and resize it as necessary. Then click the **Apply** button at the top-right

Import a List of Contacts

If you already have a list of contacts created with a different program, you can import them to People and save yourself the bother of entering them manually:

1. On the Start menu, click **People**

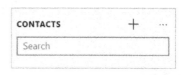

2. The app opens – click the ... button at the right and then click **Settings**

3. From Settings, click **Add an account**

4. In the **Choose an account** window, click the account or service that you want to import contacts from.

   If the account or service you want isn't there, click **Advanced set-up** at the bottom. This lets you choose accounts that use Exchange Active Sync, and POP and IMAP web-based accounts

5. Enter the email address and password for the selected account or service and then click the **Sign-in** button

6. Successful importation is indicated by a confirmation window that states the account is linked to the People app. The contacts it contains are now available under Contacts on the main window

Managing Email

Creating Folders

If you do a lot of emailing, it can be very helpful from an organizational point of view to place your messages in related folders, or mailboxes. The ability to do this is a standard feature in most email apps. Not so Window's 10 Mail app, however – this functionality is not present.

A work-around is to create the required folders in a different email app and then import them by importing the account to the Mail app as described on page 128.

Moving Messages

Having created some folders as described above, or if you are using the default folders provided with Mail, you can move messages to and from them.

To do this:

1.   Open any folder, including the Inbox, and right-click on the message to be moved

2.   From the right-click menu, select **Move**

3.   The account's folder list will open; just click on the one you want to move the message to and it's done.

Favorite Folders

By default, the Mail app provides Inbox, Drafts, Sent Items, and All Mail folders – these are shown on the folder list on the sidebar at the left. If you want access to any additional folders you have created for organization purposes, you have to click the **More** option in the app to reveal the other folders.

Some of these folders may actually be more important than the default Mail folders and so you may want these to show up in the folder list as well.

To do this:

1.   On the sidebar, click the **More** option to reveal your email folders

2.   Locate the folder you want quick access to, right-click on it and choose **Add to Favorites**

The folder will be now available from the folder list and will be placed below the default Mail app folders.

You can also use this method to "pin" any of your email folders to the Windows 10 Start menu. When done, the pinned tile will show a count of new emails that are delivered to these folders.

CHAPTER 11

Pictures, Video and Audio

Pictures and video are now produced, transported and viewed as files in a range of digital formats. With the appropriate software, your computer lets you view, edit, print, store, and organize your photos and videos. The same applies to music.

In Chapter 11, we demonstrate how to use your computer to get the best out of these activities. We also take a brief look at gaming with your Windows 10 computer.

Image Formats

There are a wide range of digital image formats. While it isn't essential to know what these are, it can be helpful on occasion. The main formats are:

BMP (Windows bitmap)
This format handles graphics files within Windows. The files are uncompressed, and therefore large, but they are widely accepted in Windows applications and so are simple to use.

GIF (Graphics Interchange Format)
This is format is limited to 256 colors. It is useful for graphics with relatively few colors such as diagrams, shapes, logos and cartoon style images. The GIF format supports animation. It also uses a lossless compression that is effective when large areas have a single color, but ineffective for detailed images or dithered images.

JPEG (Joint Photographic Experts Group)
The JPEG/JFIF filename extension is JPG or JPEG, and it uses lossy compression. Nearly every digital camera can save images in the JPEG format, which supports 24-bit color depth and produces relatively small files. JPEG files suffer generational degradation when repeatedly edited and saved.

PNG (Portable Network Graphic)
The PNG format was created as the successor to GIF. It supports trucolor and provides a lossless format that is best suited for editing pictures. Lossy formats like JPEG, on the other hand, are best for the final distribution of photographic images as they are usually smaller than PNG. PNG works well with web browsers.

Raw Image Format
The Raw Image format is used on some digital cameras to provide lossless or nearly-lossless compression. This produces much smaller file sizes than the TIFF formats from the same cameras.

Raw formats used by most cameras are not standardized or documented, and differ between camera manufacturers. Graphic programs and image editors may not accept some or all of them, so you should use the software supplied with the camera to convert the images for editing purposes, and retain the raw files as originals and backup.

TIFF (Tagged Image File Format)
This is a flexible format that saves 24-bit and 48-bit color, and uses the TIFF or TIF filename extension. TIFFs can be lossy and lossless, with some digital cameras using the LZW compression algorithm for lossless storage. TIFF is not well supported by browsers but is a photograph file standard for printing.

Photos App

Given how simple and basic it appears to be at first glance, the Photos app supplied with Windows 10 is a surprisingly powerful performer that is packed with features to help you view, edit and organize your digital images. It even lets you share your pictures via social networks and email.

The app has two main sections: Collection and Albums. In the Collection section, you'll see a collection of all your photos grouped by date taken and in reverse chronological order. If you want to quickly find photos from a certain time period without scrolling through all of the photos in your collection, click on a date to zoom out to a list of all previous months.

With regard to albums, the app will automatically create albums of photos based on the place they were taken, when they were taken, and who is in them. Photos won't let you sort by people but you can create your own albums. Also, the app will "pretty up" your albums by automatically choosing a cover image and starting off with a sample of the best or most popular pictures.

By default, the Photos app will automatically enhance photos – removing red eye, and adjusting aspects such as brightness, contrast and color. You can turn this off, however.

Potentially a very useful feature is the automatic removal of duplicate pictures. If you have thousands of photos from different devices, it's quite likely that you have a lot of duplicates from shuttling photos between those devices. This feature could save you a lot of time when organizing your collection.

Windows 10 is designed to work on both computers and mobile devices, so syncing content and settings is a priority. Windows 10's Photos app will achieve this through integration with OneDrive. OneDrive offers the first 15GB for free, with storage going up to 1TB for a small monthly fee.

Importing Pictures

The first step in using the Photos app is getting some pictures into it. Do this as follows:

1. Open the app from the Start menu and click the **Import** button at the far-right of the toolbar

2. The Photos app will search for devices likely to contain pictures that can be imported. You'll see a list of the ones it has found as shown below:

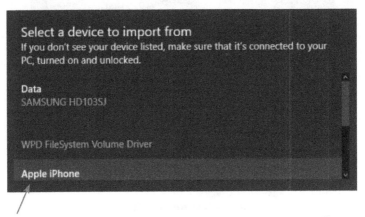

3. Select the required device. If it contains new pictures, you will see an Import button. Click it to start importing – a progress indicator at the top of the screen will keep you informed

4. When the importation is complete, a **Finished** message will pop-up on the screen. Click **Albums** in the sidebar at the left and, at the top of the window, you will see a **Last import** folder – click this to view your imported pictures

Viewing Pictures

When viewing pictures with the Photos app, you can look at them in either the Collections view or the Albums view.

If you select the former, you are presented with a scrollable list of all your pictures, starting with the most recent. If you choose the latter, you get a list of albums, again, starting with the most recent. Click on an album to open a list of the pictures it contains.

Having clicked on a picture to open it, at the top-left you will see a toolbar offering a number of options (click once on the picture to hide the toolbar).

From left to right, these are:

- **Share** – this opens a list of apps with which the picture can be shared

- **Slideshow** – clicking Slideshow will start a full-screen slideshow

- **Enhance** – the Enhance button applies automatic image correction

- **Edit** – clicking the Edit button opens a wide range of tools with which to edit the picture – we look at these on page 142

- **Rotate** – this rotates the picture in 90 degree steps

- **Delete** – click the Delete button to get rid of the picture

- **See more** – this button provides more options. You can specify a different app for opening pictures of this type, you can copy it, you can print it, and you can set it as wallpaper for both the Desktop and the Lock screen

Hovering the mouse over the bottom-right corner will reveal + and - buttons that let you zoom in and out. You can also double-click on a picture to zoom in.

Editing Pictures

One of the great things about computers is the way they allow you to play about with pictures. You can blow them up, cut bits out of them, digitally enhance and alter them, and then use the finished result in any number of ways. This can be both for business and for fun. Whatever your reason for doing it, the Photos App supplied with Windows 10 provides you with the means.

Open the picture to be edited and click the **Edit** button on the toolbar as explained on the previous page. You will then see the editing tools appear on the left side of the picture with the options for each tool on the right.

Basic fixes

The first tool is actually several tools in one. At the right, you'll see **Enhance** and **Rotate**, which we've already mentioned.

Next is **Crop** – this tool places a handle at each corner of the image with which you can "crop" out unwanted parts of the picture.

One example of how this can be used is to effectively zoom in on a particular feature in a picture.

Straighten lets you straighten a picture that has been taken at an angle relative to the horizon. At the right of the picture, you'll see a compass with a white blob to the side – drag the blob to adjust the angle.

The **Red eye** tool lets you remove the red eye effect where it is present. Move the circle over the affected eye and click to remove it. Finally, there is the **Retouch** tool, which can be used to remove small marks and blemishes by clicking on them.

Filters
The filters tool gives you six built-in filters. These let you make instant changes to the look of a picture – black & white, for example

Light
Clicking Light opens four options on the right of the picture. These let you adjust the picture's light level, contrast, highlights and shadows. These adjustments can improve the look of a picture by a considerable degree.

Color
Color tools include Temperature, Tint, Saturation and Color boost. As with the Light tools, judicious use of these tools can take a so so photo and make it look like it was taken by a pro. Overuse will have the opposite effect!

Effects
Effects offers two tools. The **Vignette** tool creates a drop-shadow effect around the edges of the picture giving it an "arty" feel.

The **Selective focus** tool effectively highlights a section of a picture by keeping it in focus and blurring the rest of it. This can be used to create a range of photographic effects.

As you make your edits, buttons will appear on the toolbar that let you save a copy of the edited picture, apply the edits to the original, and undo them.

Video Formats

As with pictures, there are many types of video format. For people who intend to work with video on their computer, it is well worth knowing the pros and cons of the most commonly used types. These are:

AVI (Audio Video Interleave

Developed by Microsoft, the AVI format is one of the oldest video formats. It is so universally accepted that many people consider it the de facto standard for storing videos on the computer. Due to it's simple architecture, AVI files are able to run on a number of different systems like Windows, Macintosh, and Linux.

WMV (Windows Media Video)

Designed for web streaming applications, WMV files are the smallest video files used on the web as their file size decreases significantly after compression. This makes it an ideal format for uploading and sharing videos via social media sites such as FaceBook.

MOV (Apple QuickTime Movie)

Developed by Apple, the QuickTime file format is a popular type of video sharing and viewing format amongst Macintosh users, and is often used on the web and for saving video files. MOV files are not just limited to Apple computers – there is a free version of the QuickTime Player available for Windows. Considered one of the best looking file formats, MOV files are of high quality and are usually large.

MPEG4 (Moving Pictures Expert group 4)

The MPEG4 video format uses separate compression for audio and video tracks – video is compressed with MPEG-4 or H.264 video encoding, while audio is compressed using AAC compression. File sizes are relatively small but the quality is high even after compression. The format is now becoming more popular than FLV for online video sharing, as it compatible with both online and mobile browsers and is supported by HTML5.

FLV (Flash Video Format)

FLV files can be played with the Adobe Flash Player, web browser plug-ins, and various third-party programs. Since virtually everyone has the player installed on their browser, it has become the most common online video viewing platform on the Internet today.

Almost all video sharing sites stream videos in Flash, so practically all browsers support, and are compatible with, the FLV format.

Movies & TV App

Window 10's Movies & TV app brings the latest HD movies and TV shows to your Windows 10 device.

It enables you to rent and buy new blockbuster movies and favorite classics, or catch up on last night's TV. Movies & TV also brings you instant-on HD and fast access to your video collection.

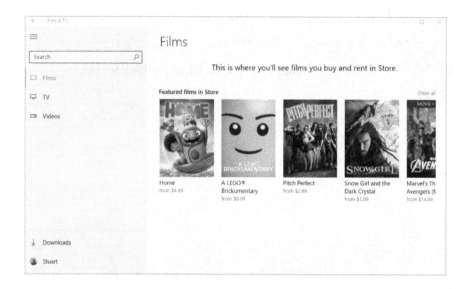

With it, you can:

- Rent and buy the latest movies on your Windows 10 device

- Get the latest TV shows the day after they air

- Use customer and critic ratings when choosing programs

- Watch purchases and rentals on your Xbox 360, Xbox One, Windows 10 device, Windows Phone, and on the Internet

- Find what you're looking for quickly and easily

- Get detailed descriptions of your favorite movies and TV shows

- Use closed captioning – this is available for most movies and TV shows

The Movies & TV app plays most DRM-free videos with the following file extensions: M4, MPEG4, MOV, ASF, AVI, WMV, M2TS, 3G2, 3GP2 and 3GPP.

Importing Video

When you first open the Movies and TV app, it searches your computer for compatible videos. It doesn't look just in the default Windows video folder, which is C:\Users\Public\Videos, it looks everywhere.

Whichever folder it finds a video in, it will continue to watch that folder in case more videos are added to it. To see what folders the app is monitoring:

1. Open the app from the Start menu

2. On the sidebar at the left, click **Settings**

3. In the **Your videos** section, click **Choose where we look for videos**

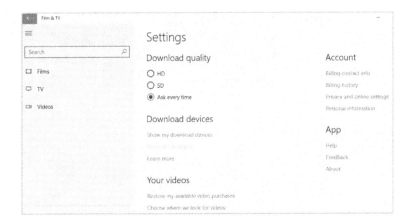

4. The window that opens shows you the folders the app is watching

5. You can click the + button and designate a different folder, or more folders, to be monitored. You can remove the currently monitored folders by clicking the **X** at the top-right

From this, you can see that videos aren't actually imported as such – the app's video list is simply a list of shortcuts to the videos. On the app's main screen, click **Videos** on the sidebar to see a thumbnailed list of the videos on the computer.

Buying & Downloading Video

If you intend to watch movies and TV on your computer, the Windows Store is one of the places you can get them from. Do it as follows:

1. On the Movies and TV app's sidebar, click **Shop for more** at the bottom

2. The Windows Store will open at the **Movies & TV** section

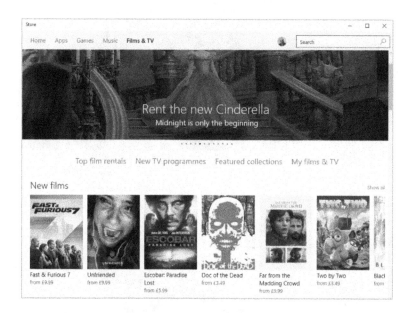

3. At the top of the screen, you will see new movies and top-selling movies. As you scroll down the window, you'll see sections for featured movies, new TV programs, top-selling TV programs, featured TV programs, top-rated TV programs and featured collections. Right at the bottom is a list of movie genres

4. Click on an item to see detailed information about it. This usually includes a free trailer, a synopsis, the price, and the cast and crew. There may also be reviews and ratings from people who have already watched it

5. When you're ready to buy, click the **Buy** or **Rent** button. A window will open offering options to either stream the movie or to download it to the computer to watch offline. Make your choice and click **Next**

6. The next window will ask you to enter your Microsoft password. Do so and click the **Sign in** button

7. Enter your payment details and the movie will then be downloaded or streamed

Playing a Video or Movie

To play an item, be it a home video or a movie downloaded from the Windows Store, open the Movies & TV app.

1. On the sidebar, click the relevant section – Movies, TV or Videos

2. Click on the movie you want to play

3. The movie opens in a new window with the playback controls at the bottom

Setting Up Your Speakers

Most desktop and laptop computers are equipped with audio facilities that are capable of producing high fidelity audio playback. On desktop machines, the sound card or motherboard will provide the connections for the various types of speaker setup. These range from simple stereo speakers to multiple speaker sets with surround sound.

For a laptop or notebook, the options are often limited to microphone and headset sockets, though some laptops include more sophisticated connections such as the SPDIF (Sony Philips Digital Interface) used for home theater connections.

You may have speakers attached to your computer, or built into the casing of a portable computer. To check it out:

1. Open the Control Panel (right-click on the **Start** button and click **Control Panel**)

2. In the Control Panel, click **Sound**

3. Click **Speakers** and then click **Configure**

4. Select your configuration, click **Next** and follow the prompts to finish and save the speaker configuration

Groove & the Groove Music App

Groove is Microsoft's newly branded music service and has risen out of the ashes of Xbox Music. While the core of the service remains the same, with the launch of Windows 10, Groove is now available to millions around the world.

Groove music is the app while Groove is the service. With a Groove music pass, you get access to Microsoft's catalog of online music to stream or download for offline use. The pass is valid on Windows 10 as well as Windows Phone, iOS, Android, Xbox and the web, with prices per month varying per region. Signing up does require a Microsoft account, though if you're using Windows 10 you've probably already got one.

As with most other streaming services, your Groove music pass lets you subscribe to unlimited on-demand music from a huge catalog for $9.99 per month. But unlike the other services, Groove lacks a free, ad-supported listening option. If you don't want to pay for the subscription, however, you can still upload your music files to OneDrive to have them available for playing in Groove. You can also purchase songs and albums outright, usually for 99 cents and $9.99, respectively.

If you want to download the music for offline listening, there are a couple of things to be aware of:

1. You can only have offline music on a total of five devices at any one time. So be sure to head into your account (through the settings menu in Groove) and ensure any old devices have been deactivated. You can only remove one every 30 days

2. Whether you've got a collection of personal music from your own sources or amassed through online stores like iTunes and Google Play, the Groove app on Windows 10 will catalog it and play it for you. In most cases, all you need to know is where on your computer the music is stored and tell the app where to find it

Groove doesn't just allow you to stream music from its online catalog; you can also create your own personal cloud locker with OneDrive. By adding your music to OneDrive, you can get the Groove or Xbox Music apps to play it on all your devices.

Whether you have a Groove music pass or not, you may find yourself wanting to purchase tracks to listen to. This is now done through the Windows Store. You can either go directly to the Store app on your computer or tablet and press the Music tab or through the Groove app.

Importing Music

Getting music into the Groove Music app is done as follows:

1. Open Groove and click the **Settings** button at the bottom of the sidebar

2. Under **Music on this PC**, click **Choose where we look for music**

3. In the new window, you'll see a list of folders that the app is using to build its music collection. As with the Movies & TV app, these include the standard Windows folders for files of this type

4. Click the + button to open File Explorer and browse to a folder containing music that you want to add to the app. Select it and then click the **Add this folder to Music** button. Repeat for any other folders you want to add

5. As you add more music to the folders being watched by Groove, it will be imported automatically

Playing Music

Having got some music into the Groove app, you have three ways to view it: by album, by artist and by song – make your choice from the top of the sidebar. In the example below, we have selected the Songs view and clicked on a song to start it playing.

The playback controls are at the bottom of the screen and are the standard Play, Pause, Back, Forward, Shuffle and Repeat.

Playlists

A useful feature in the Groove app is Playlists. A playlist is a list of songs that can be played in sequential or shuffled order. Create one as follows:

1. Click **New playlist** on the sidebar

2. A window will open in which you enter a name for the playlist

3. The playlist is created and added to the **Playlist** section on the sidebar

4. Go through your music collection and right-click on any song you want to add to the playlist – select **Add to** and then click the required playlist

To play the playlist, click on it in the sidebar.

We've explained how to get the music on your computer into the Groove app. There's also the option of buying and downloading music from the Windows Store. To do this, click the **Get music in Store** link at the bottom of the sidebar – the procedure for browsing and buying music is exactly the same as for video.

Don't forget to check out the app's settings – a range of options are available here.

Gaming With Windows 10

Every Windows 10 machine comes pre-loaded with the Xbox app, which is designed to be a gaming hub. A core feature is the real-time activity stream that alerts you to what your friends are playing, earning, and sharing. You're also able to see at a glance which of your friends are online, and send them both text and voice messages, making the messaging feature cross-platform.

Additionally, a list of the games you've played recently on all platforms allows you to easily pick up where you've left off, making the switch between platforms seamless.

DirectX 12
Most Xbox games are built around DirectX, so DirectX 12 means your games will run and look better than ever – a game running on the same hardware improves noticeably with DirectX 12 when compared to DirectX 11.

The benefits aren't just visual, either. DirectX 12 provides developers with much more control over the CPU and GPU, resulting in up to a 50% increase in performance. The benefits extend to mobile gaming as well – with power consumption cut by up to half, mobile games run more smoothly and require less battery power.

Streaming Xbox One Games
With Windows 10, your Xbox is going to break out of its box. After linking your computer with the Xbox, you are able to stream your games to your computer via the Xbox app.

This lets you play any game on the computer. If you use a laptop, your Xbox game collection follows you from screen to screen, so you can play Halo in your bedroom, kitchen, or as far as your Wi-Fi will go.

Using the Xbox App
Get started with the Xbox by clicking the Xbox app on the Start menu.

If you're logged in to your computer with a Microsoft account, you will be automatically logged in to the Xbox app. It will open as shown below:

The app's options are on the sidebar at the left, and recent games are listed on the main part of the screen. At the top, there is a link that opens customizing options, such as your name, avatar and gamertag. At the top-right of the screen is a search box that you can use to add friends.

Microsoft Solitaire Collection

Users who want less frenetic gaming can amuse themselves with a number of games that comprise the Microsoft Solitaire Collection shown below – this is available from the Start menu

CHAPTER 12

Security

The stuff on your computer – files, contacts, programs, email, etc, doesn't just appear there by magic – it is usually the result of years of using the device. Losing it all can be nothing short of a disaster as you are then faced with the task of creating it all again.

In this chapter, we focus on how to keep your computer, and the data on it, safe and secure.

Passwords

We'll begin this chapter on the subject of passwords.

Standard Passwords

When you log on to your computer, you are asked for a password – this happens whether you are signing in with a Microsoft account or a local account – without one, you are not allowed into the computer.

Lets take a look at your options here:

1. On the Start menu, go to the Settings app > Accounts

2. Should you wish to change your current password, click **Change** under **Change your account password.** A window will open asking you to enter the current password. Do so and, in the next screen, you are asked to enter it again in the top box, and the new password in the box below. Click **Next** and then **Finish**

3. Another option available to you is using a pin number instead of a password – many people find these easier to use. Under **Pin**, click the **Add** button. Enter your current account password and then click **Next**

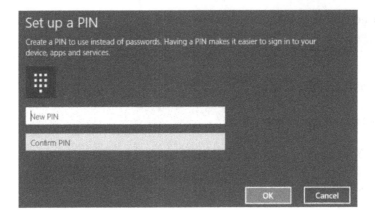

4. Enter the pin number, enter it again below to confirm, and then click **OK**. From now on, you sign in to your computer with the pin number

Picture Passwords

A more novel way of signing in to your computer is provided by the Picture password feature. This enables you to use a picture from your library as a password. You have to perform three gestures on the selected picture. To do this:

1. In the Accounts sign-in options screen, click **Add** under **Picture password**

2. In the window that opens, enter your password and click **OK**

3. At the left, click **Select picture**

4. File Explorer opens – browse to the picture you want to use

5. Draw three gestures on the picture – you can use any combination of circles, straight lines and taps

6. You'll be asked to repeat the gestures to confirm. Click **Finish** and you're done

The next time you log on to the computer, you'll see the picture. Draw the three gestures and you're in.

Windows Hello

Windows Hello is the name given to Microsoft's biometric security system for Windows 10. It employs facial- and fingerprint-recognition technology that scans your face or fingerprints when you sit down in front of the computer. If it recognizes you, the computer is unlocked.

You can get going with Windows Hello in two ways

- Purchase a laptop or tablet with the required security device built-in. This can be a special "depth" camera or a fingerprint reader

- Add the security device to an existing set up

With regard to the cameras, they are not cheap so if you want to use the Hello feature, it may be better to buy a computer with one built in.

To set up Windows Hello on your computer:

1. On the Start Menu, go to the **Settings** app and click **Accounts**

2. Set up a pin number as we explain on page 156 – this is required to use Windows Hello

3. That done, the Windows Hello settings will now be available

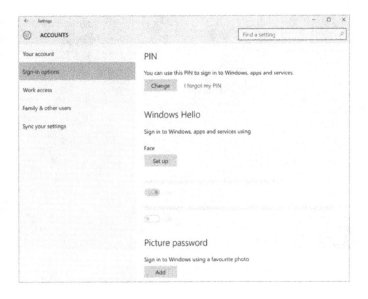

4. Click **Set up** under **Face** and then click the **Get started** button

5. From this point follow the prompts. Note that these will vary according to the security device being used

Microsoft Passport

Closely related to the Windows Hello feature, Microsoft Passport takes things a step further. Once you have signed in to your computer with Hello, you will be able to instantly access web sites and services across a range of industries, favorite commerce sites, email and social networking services, financial institutions, business networks and more – all without the need to enter a password.

The rationale behind Hello and Passport is the fact that while passwords are simple to use, they are also insecure, hard to manage, and prone to breaches and phishing attacks. To protect users from the risks of passwords, the industry has come up with a range of methods - password complexity policies, changing passwords on a set frequency, one-time passwords (OTPs), and multi-factor authentication (MFA). These all help, but at the cost of usability.

Smartcards, the other major credential method commonly used, are more secure than passwords while also providing a physical second factor. The downside is that they require considerable infrastructure to deploy and maintain. Plus, there is extremely limited support for smartcard authentication on mobile devices.

The goal with Microsoft Passport is to overcome these issues by eliminating the need for passwords. This will be done by merging the simplicity of passwords with the higher security of smartcards. If Windows Hello is not supported by the user's hardware, Passport will fall back to asking for a pin or password.

Windows Hello will store your biometric signature locally and use it for just two purposes: unlocking your Windows 10 device and using Passport.

In addition to various apps and websites, Passport will work with thousands of enterprise Azure Active Directory services at launch.

Data Encryption

Another password-related risk to the security of your data arises when your computer is stolen. The thieves may not be able to crack your password in order to gain access to the computer but they could take the hard drive out and install it in their own computer.

The solution to this problem is data encryption, and Windows 10 provides two utilities that you can use. The first of these is:

Encrypting File System (EFS)
This system encodes files and folders so they can only be read when you log on to the computer with the associated user account. During the process, an encryption key is created and stored within the user account. If an attempt is made to access the file from a different user account, the encryption key won't be available and so the file cannot be decrypted.

To encrypt a file with EFS:

1.   Open File Explorer and browse to the required folder

2.   Right-click on the folder, select the **General** tab and then click **Properties**

3.   Click the **Advanced** button

4.   In the **Advanced attributes** box, check **Encrypt contents to secure data** box and click **OK**

5.   On the **General** tab, click **Apply** and, in the **Confirm Attribute Changes** window, click **OK**

6.   Click **OK** once more and the encryption procedure begins – you will see a progress indicator as shown below

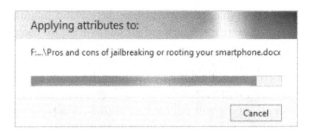

When the encryption is complete, check the folder in File Explorer. You will notice that its name text has now changed to green – this is the only indication that a folder has been encrypted. Another user logging in to your computer via a different account will be able to see and access the folder but will not be able to open the files inside it.

cont'd

BitLocker Drive Encryption

EFS is fine for encrypting folders and individual files. However, you can also choose to encrypt an entire drive. If so, you need Windows BitLocker feature.

Use it as follows:

1. Type **bitlocker** into the Taskbar search box and press **Enter**

2. The **BitLocker Drive Encryption** window opens

3. All the drives on your computer are displayed. Click on the one you want to encrypt

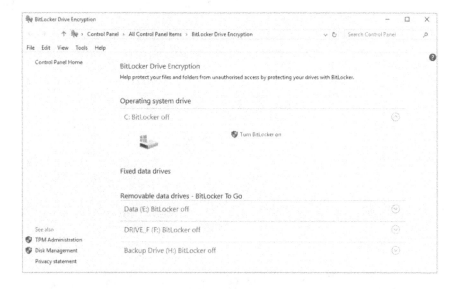

4. After initializing, a window will open asking you to enter a password with which to unlock the drive. Do so and click **Next**

5. At the next window, specify where the recovery key is to be saved and then click **Next**

6. You will now be asked if you want to encrypt the entire drive or just the part of it that's currently in use. Make your choice and click **Next**. Then in the next window, click **Start encrypting**

Once BitLocker is turned on on a drive, all data subsequently added to it is encrypted as well.

Note that the feature is only available on the Pro and Enterprise editions of Windows 10.

Sync Important Data

We've mentioned OneDrive a few times in this book and how it can be used to access and share your files from anywhere. Another way it can be used is to make sure important data is automatically saved online so if anything happens to your computer, a copy will always be available. Do it as follows:

1. Open File Explorer and browse to the folder containing the important data

2. Left-click on the folder and drag it across to the OneDrive folder on the navigation bar and release it

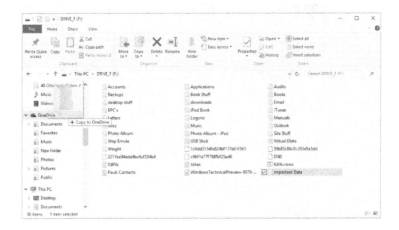

3. Now access your OneDrive at www.OneDrive.live.com

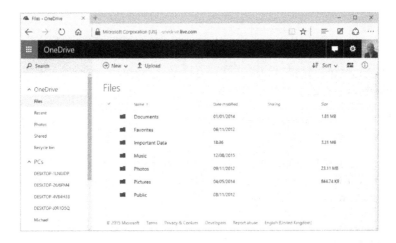

4. You will see that your folder is now safely stored online. You can now use the folder on your PC as a backup folder – any data you add to it will automatically be synced (copied) to the folder in OneDrive

Back Up Your Files

There are a number of issues that can be experienced when working with files. You may simply have lost one. Or, you may have deleted one by accident. A file can become corrupted and refuse to open. All these issues, and more, can be resolved with the Windows 10 File History utility.

Before you can use it though, you need to get a separate drive on which to store the backup. Once you have:

1. Open the Start menu and click **Settings**

2. In Settings, click **Update & Security** and then **Backup**

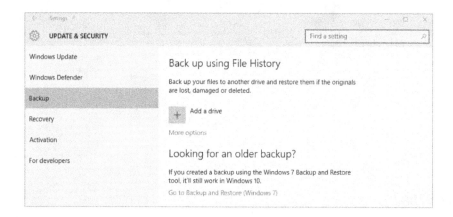

3. Click **Add a drive**. A list of available drives will appear – select the one you want to use for the backup

4. Click the **Automatically back up my files option** to **On**

5. Click **More options** and, in the new window, **click Back up now**

6. Before you exit this window, scroll down to the **Back up these folders** section. The folders listed are the ones that are backed up – make sure everything you want to backup is in one of these folders. If not, click the **Add a folder** button, browse to the required folder, select it and click the **Choose this folder** button

From this point on, File History will work silently in the background backing up the specified folders to the backup drive. By default, the backup is updated every hour, which is something you can change if you want to by opening the Backup options screen and selecting a different period. You can also specify how long Windows is to keep the backup – the default is forever but you can set it to be between one month and 2 years.

Complete System Backup

The File History utility is fine as far as it goes but it does not let you create a complete backup of your system. For this, you need to use another of Window 10's utilities, Back up and Restore.

1. Right-click on the Start button and click **Control Panel**

2. Click **Back up and Restore (Windows 7)**

3. At the left of the screen, click **Create a system image**

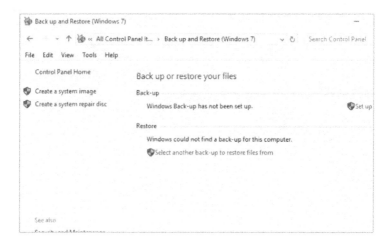

4. Windows will look for a separate drive on which to place the system image backup. You can also save it on DVD discs or to a network location. Make your choice and click **Next**

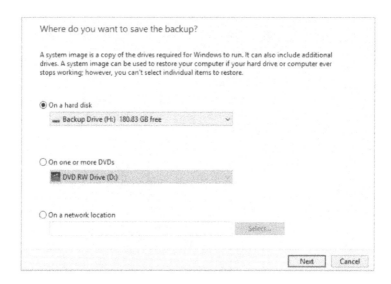

cont'd

5. At the next screen, select all the drives (assuming you have more than one) to be included in the backup

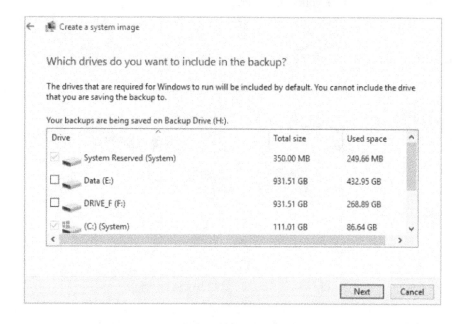

6. Click **Next** and then click **Start backup** at the final screen

Restore Your System

When your system image backup has been built (and this can take several hours), you then need to create a system repair disc, which you use with the system image to restore your computer.

To do this:

1. Open Back up and Restore (Windows 7) as previously described

2. At the left of the screen, click **Create a system repair disc**

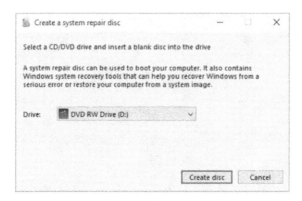

3. Make sure there is a DVD in the DVD drive and then click **Create disc.** The procedure takes just a few minutes

Restoring From a System Backup
Should you ever have reason to restore your computer from the system image backup, do the following:

1. Place the system repair disc in your DVD drive

2. Restart the computer

3. When prompted, press any key to boot the computer from the disc

4. From the recovery options displayed, select **System Image Recovery**

The computer will now be restored from the system image to how it was when the image was created – any data created since will be lost.

If you don't have a DVD drive in your PC, you can create a recovery drive instead – this uses a USB flash drive. Open the Control Panel and click **Recovery**. At the top of the window, click **Create a recovery drive** and follow the instructions. The recovery drive works in much the same way as the system repair disc – connect it to the PC, restart it, find the **System Image Recovery** option and go from there.

Antivirus Software

Antivirus software are programs designed to prevent, search for, detect, and remove software viruses, and other malicious software like worms, trojans, adware, and more.

Windows 10 provides a built-in antivirus program called Windows Defender. Access its settings at **Settings > Update & Security > Windows Defender**. The program is a fairly basic example of its type and offers just two options: an on/off switch and the ability to add exclusions.

For all that it's simple and straightforward, Windows Defender has a lot of advantages. It's built-in, won't harass you with pop-ups, and is lighter than some competing antivirus solutions. Also, it won't attempt to harvest your browsing data as some free antivirus programs have started doing in an attempt to make a profit. Plus, it's free!

Overall, Windows Defender provides reasonably good protection and will probably be fine for most PCs, along with some common sense and good security practices. However, if you're regularly downloading pirated applications and engaging in other high-risk behavior, you may want to disable Windows Defender and get something that offers a higher level of protection.

We also suggest an anti-exploit program to protect your web browser and plug-ins, which are the most targeted by attackers. **MalwareBytes Anti-Exploit** is a free program and we recommend it. It functions in a similar way to Microsoft's EMET security tool, but is more user-friendly and offers more security features that help block common exploit techniques.

If you are looking for something better than Windows Defender, the ones to go for are **Kaspersky AntiVirus** and **BitDefender**. Both are consistently ranked at the top of the detection rate charts.

If you do install a third-party antivirus program, Windows Defender will automatically disable itself and then re-enable itself if you ever uninstall the third-party program.

Privacy Issues in Windows 10

Personal privacy is a serious concern for anyone who surfs, shops or banks online. Google, Facebook, advertisers, hackers and others are all constantly trying to get your information so they can make money out of you.

This includes Microsoft. With every version of Windows, it's digging further and further into your personal life, and Windows 10 is no exception. In fact, it introduces some new features that collect your data like never before. And by default, they are all turned on. Fortunately, you can turn them off if you know where to look.

The main offenders are:

Advertising
Like every other major online company, Microsoft is using targeted advertising to increase revenue. That means it's sending advertisers your data so they know what ads to send you. While you can't shut off the advertising, you can stop advertisers from seeing what you're doing. Do this by going to **Start** > **Settings** and select **Privacy**. In Privacy, go to **General** and switch **Let apps use my advertising** ID to **Off**. Now, advertisers won't get your advertiser ID when you visit a page.

Location
Still on the Privacy screen, head to the **Location** area. Here, you can tell Windows to stop tracking your location entirely, or specify which apps can and can't use your location. Location is useful for apps like the Weather app or when you're looking at maps because you don't have to put in your address every time. However, other apps might use it to keep tabs on you.

Cortana
In order to provide you with information when requested, Cortana has to learn as much about you as possible and it does this by monitoring your movements, browsing habits, contacts, calendar and more. If you don't think you'll use Cortana, you can turn it off completely by clicking in the Taskbar search box and clicking the **Notebook** icon at the left. Then click **Settings** and turn Cortana off.

Finally, there is another setting that lets you manage what it has already learned about you. Plus, you can stop Bing from recording information about you to improve your searches.

Open the Privacy screen and under Speech, Inking & Typing, find **Getting to know you**. This controls whether or not Cortana is learning certain things about you. Turn it off by clicking **Stop getting to know me**.

CHAPTER 13

Troubleshooting & Maintenance

Your computer is a machine and, like all machines, it will go wrong from time to time. Windows provides a number of tools that can help you diagnose and repair most problems, and in this chapter we show you what they are and how to use them.

A related issue is maintenance. If you don't keep your computer properly maintained, its performance will be adversely affected. Read on to find out how to keep it running smoothly.

Isolating The Problem

Troubleshooting, whatever is being investigated, can be approached in various ways. With computers, probably the most common is the "flailing around" method. This is where the user, who almost certainly has little or no knowledge of what goes inside their computer's casing, starts frantically clicking this, that and the other in the desperate hope that, somehow, it just might do the trick.

Unfortunately, it almost never does. An approach that is far more likely to produce results, is the considered approach in which you actually think about what has just happened (or not happened, as the case may be). In almost all cases, this will enable you to narrow down the potential causes of the problem and thus vastly increase the chances of actually finding it.

Things to consider include:

- **Error messages** – it is an unfortunate fact that the majority of computer error messages are either just phrased rather badly or are totally incomprehensible. Many of them do, however, contain error codes that can be useful as in the example below

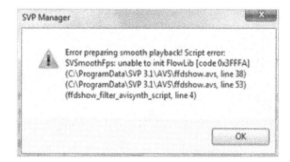

Try doing an Internet search for the code and see what comes up – usually other people somewhere in the world have experienced the same problem and you may get the solution this way. Another is to quote the code to a support technician

- **Windows settings** – Windows is chockful of things you can click. Think back – did you recently change anything? If you did and the problem showed up afterwards, you immediately have a good line of attack. If you can remember what it was that you changed, reverse that change and see what happens

- **Program settings** – computer faults are not restricted to Windows – the programs on it are just as likely to give trouble. If you recently changed something on a program that is now misbehaving, reverse the change. If the problem is still there, check to see if an update is available for the program

- **New software** – installing software on your computer is a common way of screwing it up. Most programs are fine but there are plenty of others out there that are anything but. The best move you can make whenever you are experiencing issues is to restart the computer – this action resets internal settings and can resolve a whole host of issues.

  If the problem is still present, use the computer for a while without running the program – if the problem goes away, you know what's causing it. Before giving up on the program and uninstalling it, make sure the version you have installed is compatible with Windows 10 – if not look for an updated version. If all else fails though, you will have to uninstall the program

- **Software update** – downloading and installing updates to existing programs can also be the cause of issues. One method of checking this is to use the Windows File History feature to revert to a previous version as we explained on pages 163-164. If the problem is still there afterwards though, uninstall the update.

  Unlikely as it may seem, this advice also apples to Windows itself. Windows 10 downloads and installs updates automatically (although you can put a stop to this behavior in the settings). If a problem suddenly springs up immediately after a Windows update, the update has to be suspect.

  Check it out in the Control Panel by opening the **Programs and Features** utility. On the sidebar at the left, click **View installed updates**. You will now see all the updates and the dates they were installed. To uninstall one, right-click on it and click **Uninstall**

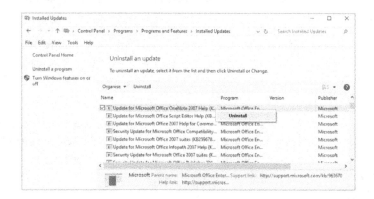

- **Device drivers** – installing hardware devices on your computer can cause problems if the device's driver is incompatible. This particular issue is easily resolved with the Windows System Restore utility – see page 175

General Troubleshooting Steps

If you follow the advice just given, you will usually be able to narrow the fault down to its approximate location. Feeling pleased with yourself, you may now be tempted to dive in and fix it.

However, before you get carried away, there are a number of very simple steps you can take that may well resolve the issue without you having to get your hands dirty.

- **Shut everything down**
  – by this, we don't mean
  Windows – just close
  all running applications.
  Every app that is open
  is using system resources
  such as memory and
  processor cycles.

  Shutting these programs
  down releases the resources and can have a dramatic effect on the computer.
  To do this, open the **Task Manager** (right-click on the Start button and
  click Task Manager). You will see a list of the programs currently running.
  Just click on them and then click the **End task** button

- **Reboot the computer** – rebooting closes all the software running on your
  computer – not only the programs you see running on the Taskbar, but also
  dozens of services that might have been started by various programs and
  never stopped. The whole system is then reloaded. Doing this will often fix
  mysterious performance problems, the exact cause of which is difficult to
  pinpoint

- **Restart the computer** – turning the computer off for a minute or so and
  then starting it up again is a well-known method of resolving hardware
  conflicts. The short period the computer is off gives the devices time to shut
  down properly

- **Connections** – a surprising amount of computer problems aren't really
  problems at all – it's just that the user has forgotten to flick the switch that
  turns a device on. On a similar vein, incorrect, missing or flaky connections
  are also common – check the cable is securely connected, and connected to
  the right device

- **Troubleshooters** – Windows 10 provides a number of automated
  troubleshooters that can check (and also resolve) various types of problem.
  We take a closer look at these on page 176

Restoring Your Files

On page 163, we explained how the File History utility can be used to create backups of your files. Here, we will explain how to use it to restore a missing or damaged file

The way to do it is:

1. Open File Explorer and navigate to the folder where you need to recover a file

2. On the folder's ribbon toolbar, click **History**. Alternatively, right-click on the folder and click **Restore previous versions**

3. In the window that opens, click the **Previous Versions** tab

4. You will now see a list of all the File History versions of the folder

5. Select the one you want to restore from

6. Click the down-arrow to the right of the Open button

7. Click **Open** in File History

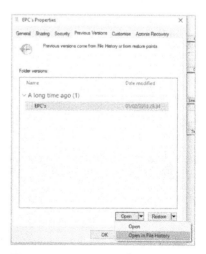

cont'd

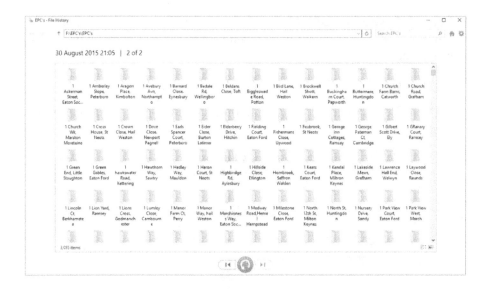

8. If the folder contains subfolders, click on it and the subfolders will be revealed as shown above. Click on a subfolder to open it and keep drilling down until you get to the file to be restored.

9. Click the **Restore to original location** button. If you want to restore all the files in a folder, select them all before clicking the Restore button

System Restore

What is System Restore?

System Restore is a Windows feature that lets you revert your computer's state (including system files, installed applications, Windows Registry, and system settings) to that of a previous point in time. This lets you recover from system malfunctions or other serious problems.

For example, the installation of a program or a driver can cause an unexpected change to your computer or cause Windows to behave unpredictably. Usually, uninstalling the program or driver corrects the problem. If uninstalling doesn't fix the problem however, you can try restoring your computer's system to an earlier date when everything worked correctly.

System Restore uses a feature called system protection to regularly create and save restore points on your computer. These restore points contain information about registry settings and other system information that Windows uses. You can also create restore points manually.

Enabling System Restore

To enable System Restore:

- Type **system restore** into the Taskbar search box and press **Enter**

- The System Properties window opens at the System Protection tab. Under Protection Settings, click **Configure**

- Tick the **Turn on system protection** radio button

System Restore will now automatically create restore points whenever potentially damaging changes are made to the system. These can then be used to "undo" these changes if necessary.

To create a restore point manually, open the System Properties window as described above and click the **Create** button.

Using System Restore

Open the System Properties window as explained above. Under the System Protection tab, click the **System Restore** button. You will now see a list of all the restore points that have been made. Choose one made prior to the fault manifesting itself, click **Next** and then click **Finish**. When the restore procedure is complete, the computer will reboot back into Windows. System Restore can also be used from a system repair disc and a recovery drive.

Note that System Restore isn't intended for backing up personal files, so it cannot help you recover a personal file that has been deleted or damaged. Use the File History utility for this purpose.

Windows Troubleshooters

Windows provides a number of troubleshooters that can help to diagnose problems. In some cases, they can even fix the problem.

To access the troubleshooters:

1. Right-click on the **Start** button and click **Control Panel**

2. Click **Troubleshooting**

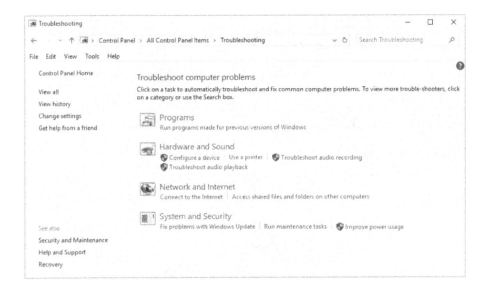

3. You will see four categories of troubleshooters – Programs, Hardware and Sound, Network and Internet, and System and Security

4. Open the most likely category

5. An online check will be made to make sure the selected troubleshooter is up-to-date

6. You will now see a list of troubleshooters for the selected category. Click the one you want to try

7. Start the troubleshooter by clicking the **Next** button

8. From this point, follow the prompts

Problem Steps Recorder

A common problem when trying to explain a fault to a support technician is making sense. The technician will want to know the nature of the problem, and a detailed description of anything you have done in an attempt to rectify it. Recalling precisely what has been done can be difficult for someone who knows about computers, so for someone who doesn't, it can be virtually impossible.

The solution is a little-known tool in Windows called Problem Steps Recorder. When run, the recorder will automatically capture all the steps you take on a computer, including a text description of where you clicked and a picture of the screen during each click (called a screenshot). Having captured these steps, you can save them to a file that can be used by a support professional.

So the next time you have a problem, record your steps as follows:

1. Type **problem steps** into the Taskbar search box and press **Enter**

2. The recorder opens as shown below:

3. Click the **Start Record** button

4. Now do whatever you can to make it in order to make it as clear as possible what the problem is

5. When you finished, click **Stop Record**

6. A screen will now open showing a step-by-step list of every single thing you did. Included will be screenshots as we see below:

7. Click the **Save** button at the top-left to save the file to a location that can be set in the utility's settings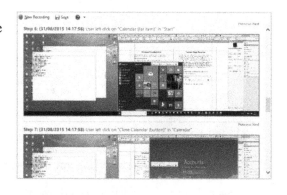

8. After saving the file, you can then send it by email. Click the **Help** down-arrow and then click **Send to E-mail recipient.** This will open an email message in your default email program with the recorded file attached to it

Windows Recovery Environment

What is it?

On page 166, we described how to make a system repair disc and a recovery drive. These are necessary in order to restore a computer from a system image backup. When used, they both boot the computer into what's known as the Windows Recovery Environment.

The RE is essentially a simplified, scaled-back version of Windows, and is used to boot the system when it cannot boot normally or run in a stable manner. Within the recovery environment, a number of recovery tools are available that can be used to diagnose and repair problems with Windows. For example, automatic repair and troubleshooting tools can test disk and file integrity. They are often able to fix common disk problems and restore files damaged by disk failures, malware activity or user errors.

Accessing the Windows Recovery Environment

There are a number of ways to access the RE and the avenue you take is largely dependant on the problem you are experiencing. If you can still get into Windows, you can do it from Update & Security:

1. Open the Start menu and click **Settings**

2. Click **Update & Security**

3. Click **Recovery**

4. Under Advanced start-up, click **Restart now**

5. The computer will now reboot into the recovery environment

If, however, you cannot get into Windows, you need to access the recovery environment as described on page 180.

Reset the Computer

In a situation whereby you are experiencing minor issues with your computer that do not warrant the rigmarole of restoring from a backup, Windows provides a tool that may be just the thing you need.

This is the Reset utility. Reset gives you a quick and easy way to start with a clean slate while, at the same, time maintaining your apps, data, Windows settings, and user profiles. Reset automatically sets aside your data, Windows settings, and apps, then puts them back where they belong once the operating system is reinstalled. The result is a clean slate for Windows, but with your configuration settings and data intact.

To reset your computer:

1. Open the Start menu and click **Settings**

2. Click **Update & Security**

3. Click **Recovery**

4. Under **Reset this PC**, click **Get started**

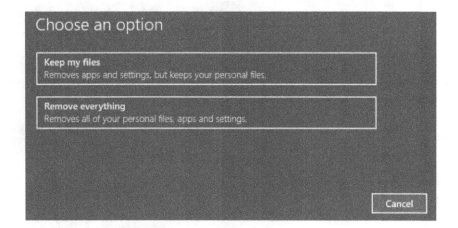

5. You are presented with two options: **Keep my files** and **Remove everything**. Select the first option and click **Reset** in the next screen

The computer will now reboot to the desktop. Note that the **Keep my files** option will not restore the software you have installed. It will restore Windows 10 apps, but not traditional Win32 software. This is to avoid re-installing software that might be the cause of the problem.

An HTML file listing the applications that were not installed is placed on the desktop so you know what software is missing.

The second option offered by Reset is **Remove everything.** This removes everything on your computer – files, apps and settings, and results in a brand new installation of Windows.

For situations where you cannot get into Windows to access the Reset utility, you need to use the Windows Recovery Environment and either a system repair disc or a USB recovery drive.

Assuming a USB recovery drive is being used, the procedure is:

1. Connect the USB drive to a USB port on the computer

2. Restart the computer

3. At the bottom of the first boot screen, press the key that opens the boot menu – this is usually the F12 key

4. When the boot menu opens, select the USB flash drive

5. You may now see a screen asking you to select your language – do so

6. You should now be in the Windows Recovery Environment or see an option that leads to it

7. Click **Troubleshoot**

8. Click **Reset this PC**

9. Click **Remove everything**

Going back to the **Choose an option** screen, you will see an Advanced options link.

This opens a screen offering a number of troubleshooting options that include System Restore, System Image recovery, Start-up Repair, Command Prompt, and Start-up Settings.

Disk Cleanup

Disk Cleanup is a Microsoft software utility first introduced with Windows 98 and included in all subsequent releases of Windows. It allows users to remove files that are no longer needed or that can be safely deleted, especially files that may not be obvious to you such as temporary files used by Windows or when browsing the Internet.

Use it as follows:

1. Type **disk cleanup** into the Taskbar search box and press **Enter**

2. The utility opens as shown at the right

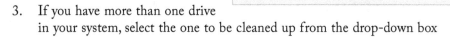
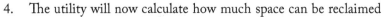

3. If you have more than one drive in your system, select the one to be cleaned up from the drop-down box

4. The utility will now calculate how much space can be reclaimed

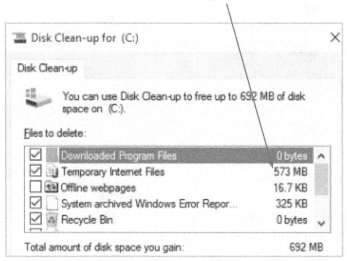

5 A window will open showing the location of the files to be deleted. You can deselect any of these by unchecking the box at the front

6. Click **OK** and the selected files will be removed from the system

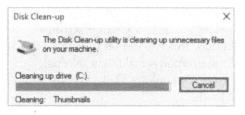

Optimize Your Drives

Defragmenting your hard drive is an integral part of keeping your PC healthy. The Optimize Drives defragmentation utility provided by Windows is very simple to use and can give a considerable boost to your PC's performance.

For the uninitiated, fragmentation is a phenomenon that causes drive storage space to be used inefficiently, reducing capacity or performance, and often both.

Open and run the utility as follows:

1. Type **optimize** into the Taskbar search box and press **Enter**

2. The Optimize Drives utility will open

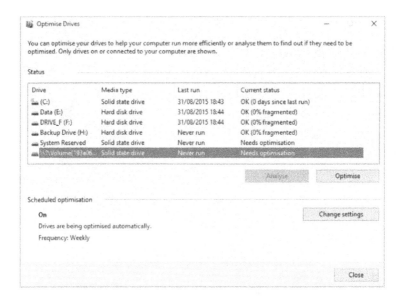

3. You will see all the drives in your system and their current defragmentation status

4. Select a drive and click **Analyse** to see if it requires optimizing

5. If it does, click the **Optimize** button

Below, you'll see a **Change settings** button. This lets you set up an Optimization schedule on selected drives. Options are Daily, Weekly and Monthly.

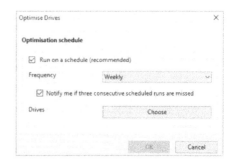

ReadyBoost

ReadyBoost is a feature that uses external USB flash drives as a hard drive cache to improve disk read performance. Supported external storage types include USB flash drives, SD cards, and CF cards.

ReadyBoost works in conjunction with a utility called SuperFetch, which monitors the programs you use on your computer and automatically loads them into your computer's memory (RAM) ahead of time. As a result, when you launch an application, it will start more quickly because the computer reads its files from the faster memory rather than the slower hard drive.

However, SuperFetch can also work with USB flash drives, which is where ReadyBoost comes in. When you connect a USB drive to your computer and enable ReadyBoost, Windows will store SuperFetch data on the USB drive, thus freeing up system memory.

It's faster to read numerous small files from the USB drive than it is to read them from the hard drive, so this can theoretically improve your system's performance.

There is, however, a catch – USB storage is slower than memory. Therefore, ReadyBoost only helps if your computer doesn't have enough memory. By "enough memory", we mean 2 GB or less – if it has more, enabling ReadyBoost is unlikely to have any noticeable effect.

So before you enable ReadyBoost, you need to establish how much memory your computer has. This can be done by going to the Control Panel and opening the System utility. In the System section, you will see the installed amount.

Once you are sure it is worth doing, enable ReadyBoost as follows:

1.   Connect a USB drive to the computer

2.   Go to This PC, right-click on the drive and click **Properties**

3.   Click the **ReadyBoost** tab

4.   Click **Apply**

The USB drive will now be used by Windows to store SuperFetch data, which in turn will release a proportional amount of system memory.

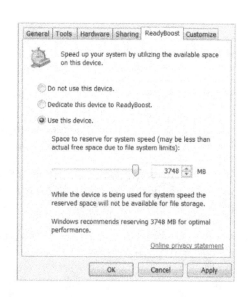

Performance Enhancement Tools

More performance enhancement tools can be found by going to the Control Panel and clicking **System**. In the System window, click **Advanced system settings at** the left. Finally, click the **Settings** button in the Performance section to open the screen below:

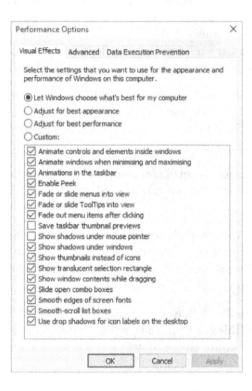

At the top are four options, and in the section below are all the visual effects used on the computer. These all make a hit on its performance so disabling any that you don't need will give you a slight boost in speed.

The **Let Windows choose what's best for my computer** option will turn on most of the visual effects. **Adjust for best appearance** turns on all the effects, while **Adjust for best performance** turns them all off. The final option, **Custom**, lets you choose which effects to turn on.

Click the **Advanced** tab and you will see options for allocating processor resources and virtual memory. With regard to the processor, you can set it for the best performance of **Programs** or of **Background services**.

Virtual memory is a paging area that Windows creates on the PC's drive and uses as extra memory. If you know what you are doing, you can adjust the size of this file; if you don't, we recommend you leave well alone.

Make Old Programs Work With Windows

With Windows 10 being a brand new operating system, many programs designed for use with the older technologies found in previous editions of Windows, are going to struggle with it. This is a well known issue and is called program incompatibility.

Compatibility Modes

To overcome this problem, Windows provides a Compatibility modes feature that basically tricks programs into thinking they're running on the version of Windows they were designed for. Many old Windows programs will run fine when using this mode, when otherwise they wouldn't.

Windows 10 will automatically enable compatibility options if it detects an application that needs them, but you can enable these compatibility options yourself as we explain below:

1. Open the program's folder and locate its executable file (.exe)

2. Right-click on the .exe file and click **Properties** at the bottom

3. Open the **Compatibility** tab

4. Your first move is to run the compatibility troubleshooter. This will give you two options: try recommended settings or to troubleshoot the program by choosing compatibility settings based on the problems you're having with it

5. If neither option does the trick, check the **Run this program in compatibility mode for** checkbox and, from the drop-down box, select the required edition of Windows

6. Click **Apply** and then **OK**

If the program still doesn't run properly, either get an updated version (if available) or thank it for all its hard work and retire it.

System Information

Troubleshooting often requires detailed information about what's being investigated – this also applies to computers. Windows gives you two types of information – basic and detailed:

Basic

For a brief summary of the main elements in your system, open the Control Panel and click **System**:

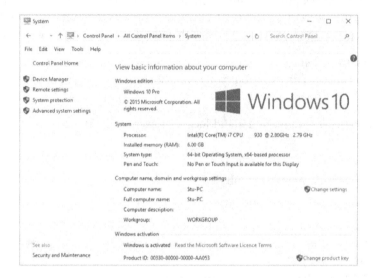

Detailed

If you need detailed information about your system, or part of, open System Information by typing **system** into the Taskbar search box and pressing **Enter**:

Index

E

F

R

S

T

U

V